# THE BATTLE OF CAMPBELL STATION

## THE SIEGE OF KNOXVILLE, THE BATTLE OF CHATTANOOGA AND CHICKAMAUGA, AND OTHER ACTION.

**As reported in the December 7, 1863 Issue of the**

## New-York Daily Tribune

**Transcribed by:**
**Charles A. Reeves, Jr.**
**Cover Painting Courtesy of:**
**Paul J. Long**
**(used with permission)**

Booklet Produced By:

**Charles A. Reeves, Jr.**
Technical Illustration & Publishing
*Specializing in Cartography and Genealogy*

10812 Dineen Drive (865) 966-5768
Knoxville, Tennessee 37934-1809
e-mail: reevesca@tds.net
Home Page: http://ReevesMaps.com

ISBN 978-0-9800984-0-2

Reproductions/Enlargements of any image in this booklet are available from Charles A. Reeves, Jr., with the exception of the Battle of Campbell Station painting. Prints are available directly from the artist:

Paul J. Long
101 N Farnum Street
Friendsville, TN 37737-2701
e-mail: pjlong@adelphia.net

How this booklet was produced: The original copy of the newspaper was scanned at 300 dpi and the images edited in Adobe Photoshop to remove artifacts. The scanned images were then converted into text using OmniPage Pro, although due to the small size and poor quality of the original, considerable clean-up was required. The text files were edited in WordPerfect, and final layout was done in Adobe Illustrator. All work was done on an Apple Macintosh G5, dual 2-Ghz computer.

# THE FIGHT AT CAMPBELL'S STATION.

From Our Special Correspondent.
CAMPBELL'S STATION, Monday, Nov. 16, 1863.

AMBROSE E. BURNSIDE.

Learning that the enemy had completed his pontoon below London [Loudon], and had crossed a considerable force, Gen. Burnside, on the 14th, ordered forward the 2nd Brigade of Gen. White's Division. His 1st Brigade had been ordered to Kingston several days previously. This force was accompanied by Gen. Ferrero's Division of the 9th A. C. The enemy's pickets were met and driven in three miles from London [Loudon]. General White directed Col. Chapin, who commanded the brigade, to deploy the 111th Ohio and the 13th Kentucky on the left. General White took charge of the 107th Illinois, deploying it on the right. The regiment gave three cheers for Illinois, and charged into their first fight on the double-quick, driving the enemy in confusion from the field. The whole line then pressed steadily forward through the woods skirting the river; the enemy repeated by attempting to make a stand, but as often being dislodge by the steady charge of the line. The 107th Illinois and the 13th Kentucky distinguished themselves. The enemy's loss was large, leaving his dead and wounded on the field. Prisoners, representing five different regiments of Longstreet's corps, were captured. Night compelled a halt within three-quarters of a mile from the enemy's pontoon. The last half mile we drove them, our troops were under the fire of their artillery from the opposite side of the river. The roughness of the ground prevented Gen. White from getting his artillery in position.

During the night Gen. Burnside ascertained that the enemy's force was large and that they were crossing rapidly. The order was given to move to the rear at daylight. Gen. White's division was ordered to cover the rear. He was very soon attacked by the enemy—Col. Chapin at once engaged him with the 111th Ohio Infantry, Gen. White's brigade facing about and repulsing the attack. He constantly skirmished with the enemy's advance until our column reached Loudon. Here the duty of protecting the rear was assigned to Col. Sigfried's division of the 9th Corps. He skirmished with the enemy's advance until our troops reached Lenoir, where they halted for the night. The roads were now rendered impassible by reason of the rains and the constant kneading of the heavy clay by the wheels of our long train passing animals. To continue to drag the wagons or artillery by means of the usual supply of horses was found impracticable. The wagons or artillery must be left. Gen. Burnside accordingly ordered the destruction of the transportation wagons of Gen. White's Division, and the horses to be used for moving the artillery. By these means the guns were moved with facility. This wise measure, adopted only from absolute necessity, undoubtedly saved the artillery which was in danger of being sacrificed, or he would have had to fight the enemy upon unequal ground at great disadvantage.

Morning of the 16th.—Resuming the march on the morning of the 16th, Campbell's Station ten miles distant, was reached at 11 o'clock a.m. Gen. White's division in the advance, the 9th. Army Corps covering the rear, and, as on the previous day, constantly pressed by the enemy. They attacked them heavily on the flank just before reaching Campbell's Station. Gen. Potter, as soon as it was known that the troops would be ordered to the rear, sent Col. Hartranft with Sigfried's brigades and Biddel's

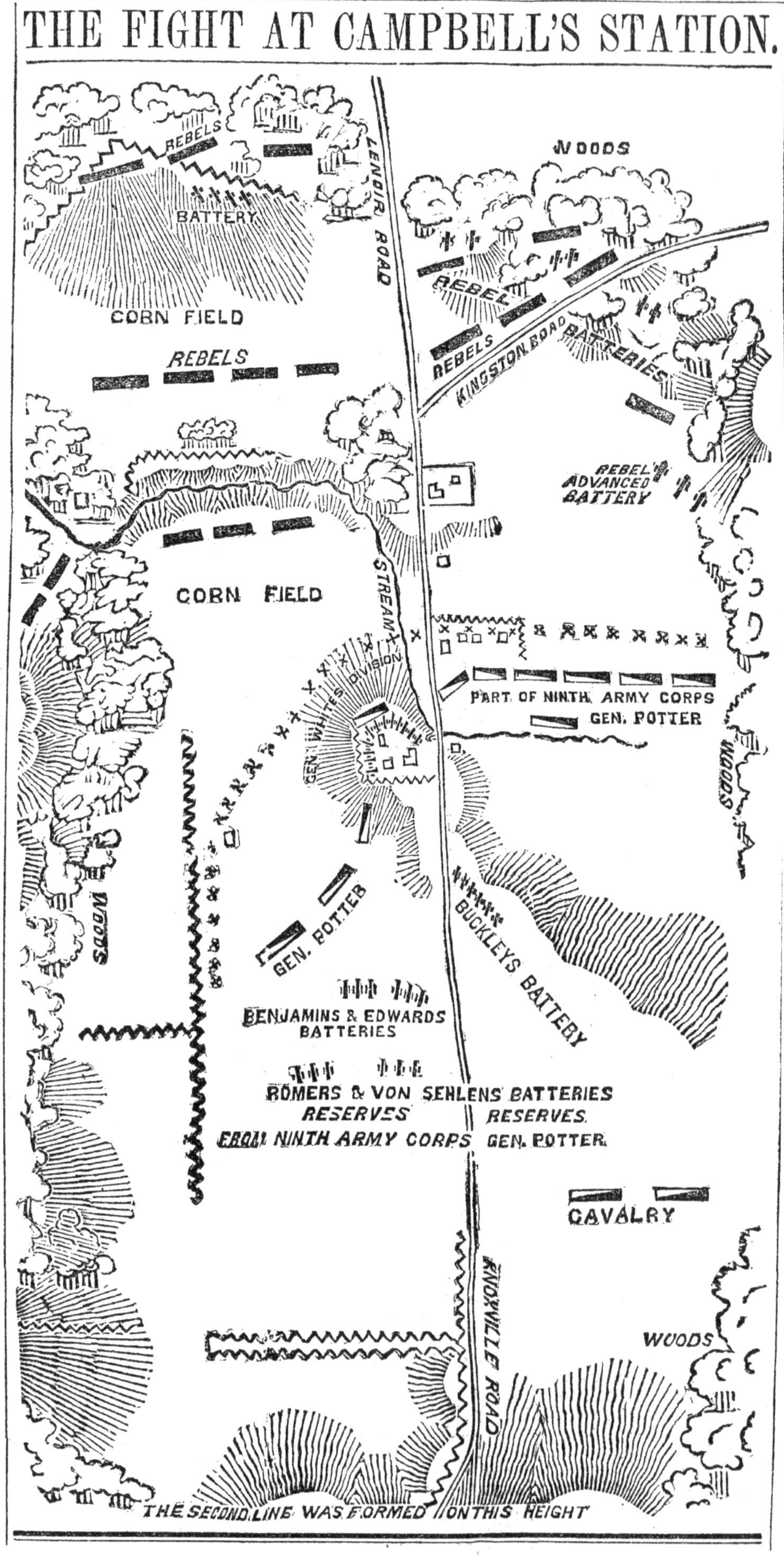
THE FIGHT AT CAMPBELL'S STATION.
REBELS
BATTERY
CORN FIELD
REBELS
LENOIR ROAD
WOODS
REBEL
REBELS
KINGSTON ROAD
BATTERIES
REBEL ADVANCED BATTERY
CORN FIELD
STREAM
GEN. WHITES DIVISION
PART OF NINTH ARMY CORPS
GEN. POTTER
WOODS
WOODS
GEN. POTTER
BUCKLEYS BATTERY
BENJAMINS & EDWARDS BATTERIES
ROMERS & VON SEHLENS BATTERIES
RESERVES
FROM NINTH ARMY CORPS
RESERVES
GEN. POTTER
CAVALRY
KNOXVILLE ROAD
WOODS
THE SECOND LINE WAS FORMED ON THIS HEIGHT

A copy of a painting by Paul J. Long—research by Jerry E. Keyes.
The original painting hangs in the Farragut, Tennessee Town Hall.



BATTLE OF CAMPBELL STATION - November 16, 1863

command of mounted men to take position covering the roads to Campbell's Station. When the head of the retiring column reached the junction of the roads from Kingston, and Lenoir, Hartranft was already engaged with the enemy on the Kingston road. Gen. White having formed his line of battle, the 9th Corps took position in the rear, Gen. Potter advancing a brigade upon the right flank and two regiments on the left of his line. At 12 o'clock the enemy appeared in great force advancing in three lines. The engagement was opened by Henshaw's Illinois Battery and the 24th Indiana Battery, and the engagement soon became general. On the arrival of the head of Ferrero's Division at the junction of the two roads, Morrison's Brigade was placed in position with his flanks resting, on each road, so that when Hartranft and Ferrero, passed by it fell back in line covering both roads.

Only a portion of the 9th and 23d Corps were out on the field, representing less than 5,000 men, which was opposed by the whole of Longstreet's Corp—how large that is, who knows? It is no doubt superior to our opposing forces.

By reference to the map I send you, the reader will obtain a tolerably correct idea of the topography of the ground where one of the most interesting [battles] of the war was fought. The battle is characterized, from beginning to close, as the "prettiest little fight" ever made. Tactical skill of the highest order was everywhere manifested by Gen. Burnside, who was everywhere at times upon the field, and by his associate in command. The movements of the troops, the station and change of batteries, and all the evolutions during the heat of battle, were according to book. A too particular account of these is not possible in the compass of this letter. After the arrival and formation of the 9th Corps, every movement, including the advance of a part of that corps, the various changes of front, and the withdrawal to the higher ground, where the second line was formed, were carried out in the most perfect manner, and with as much deliberation as if the troops had been on parade, instead of fighting the whole of Longstreet's corps. The enemy was twice repulsed, and it was only when both flanks were seriously threatened that Gen, Burnside gave the order to retire to the second position. Col. Chapin's brigade, under Gen. Potter, moved from the field in admirable order upon the ordinary quick step, while the rear-guard, under White and Chapin were well maneuvered, the rear line frequently halting fronting the enemy, and again moving forward. During the movement not a man of either corps left his proper position, although the guns of the enemy were worked with the utmost ener[g]y upon our moving column. Col. Chapin's brigade continued doing duty in the rear until the arrival of the troops at Knoxville. Contrary to expectation the enemy made no attempt to cut off our retreat.

The total losses in the fight at Campbell's Station, were as follows:

NINTH ARMY CORPS. Killed 27 Missing 71 Wounded 90 Total 163

This is exclusive of the calvary losses, which have not yet been reported.

LOSSES IN CHAPIN'S BRIGADE, TWENTY-THIRD ARMY CORPS. Killed 16 Missing (fell out sick) 5 Wounded 90 Total 121

Grand total 384

The missing in the 9th Army Corps were, many of them no doubt, taken prisoners.

E. S.

## FIGHT ON THE KINGSTON ROAD—POSITION OF THE OPPOSING FORCES—A HOT ENGAGEMENT—GALLANTRY OF OUR OFFICERS AND MEN—THE ENEMY CHARGE—GEN. SANDERS MORTALLY WOUNDED—A RASH REBEL—OUR MEN WILL FALL BACK—UNION LOSS 200.

From Our Special Correspondent. Knoxville, Nov. 18, Noon

At daylight a heavy fog hung like a gray blanket over the city and neighboring hills, obscuring all objects, and hiding friend and foe alike under its misty pall. Our soldiers rose from their herd beds fully expecting an attack, but the fog delayed the opening of the ball. At 10 o'clock the sun began to struggle through the overhanging mist, and, at a quarter to 11 a.m., the enemy's skirmishers in front on the Kingston road opened fire. They occupied a line parallel Armstrong's house, at a little over a mile, distant, and carried their batteries and a portion of their forces behind it and in the woods and ravines beyond. The enemy stretched across the road to our right, occupying a belt of timber. The ground is undulating, even hilly, and favorable for both attack and defense. Our cavalry and mounted infantry, constituting Woolford's Brigade, with ether cavalry, under command of General Sanders, had early occupied the crest of a hill about a mile in advance of our fortification on Tape Hill, to the right of the Kingston road, our line, like that of the enemy's, extending to the right, and left going about a quarter of a mile. A barricade of rails, hastily thrown up along the crest, formed the only protection for our men who lay behind this, being also partly protected by the hill slope under which their horses were hitched some distance in the rear. The enemy were covered by a line of woods. He threw his forces round to our right, and kept up a desultory fire upon our pickets toward and upon the line of the Clinton road. Col. Pennebaker of the 27th Kentucky cavalry, with the 11th mounted infantry occupied this avenue, and skirmished with the enemy's vedettes and pickets.

BRIGADIER-GENERAL WILLIAM P. SANDERS, KILLED AT KNOXVILLE. FROM A PHOTOGRAPH.

The firing opened vigorously, first from the woods. and then from the cover of the house and the enemy's rifle pits. Our men replied steadily and coolly, not man wavering or leaving his position. We had no battery in the advance, and relied chiefly upon Benjamin, whose guns were of sufficient range to reach the attacking column when the enemy were so placed as not to endanger our men. For about one hour our line of fire occupied only an eighth of a mile in extent, the enemy constantly maneuvering to get in upon our flanks. Our officers, prominent among whom could be seen Sanders, with a reckless courage, rode over the field and among the men, inspiring them and encouraging them by their example. Col. Woolford, Col. Bond, Major Dow, and, in fact, all the other officers of the three regiments engaged behaved with great gallantry, showing themselves in every part of the field where the bullets rained heaviest. A Rebel, belonging to the 15th South Carolina, who was wounded and brought to the rear, informed me, in answer to questions, that it was McClaw's division and Kershaw's brigade of South Carolina troops who were engaging us in front. Barksdale's old

Mississippi brigade was also there. From the best information I could obtain there were at least two divisions of the enemy's troops in the field. At 12 'clock, finding that our boys still hold their own and have no idea of running, the Rebels bring forward a battery of four guns which they load under cover of Armstrong's brick house, run out and fire, then withdraw again under cover. Four guns are now pouring rapid discharges of shell and grape, winds shriek, explode and plow up the groundaround them all directions. Yet our men remain as fixed as the stones, or their own breastworks. At time they arc completely hidden from view by the smoke of battle; but as the sulphurous cloud is swept away, our boys are till holding their own, as if that were the forlorn hope. Rising upon their elbows to fire, they lie down and load, then up again and deliver their fire. Now Benjamin, with his 20-pounder Parrotts, opens on the enemy's battery, and, as his well-directed shells burst among the Rebel cannoniers, a shout of satisfaction arises from our line. The Rebels at the same time fill the air with derisive shrieks and outcries, as if defying us. I observed that a pause usually followed. the treble of musketry being hushed while the bass of the opposing cannon reverberated among the hills,

The struggle was witnessed with intense interest from the various elevated positions which afforded a view of the field. The Rebel cannon now play more rapidly, and a heavy column is seen advancing from under cover of the woods. There is to be a change. As the enemy's guns are wheeled out from behind their house, a shell from our batteries goes shrieking into their midst, bursting at the feet of the Rebel gunners, which covers them with smoke and dirt. Thus the contact continued until 1 o'clock p.m., neither party seeming to have gained any advantage. Exclamations of surprise and admiration are heard on every hand that few comparatively fresh troops behave with such steadiness and intrepidity.

## THE CHARGE—GENERAL SANDERS MORTALLY WOUNDED.

About 3 o'clock p.m. a whole brigade advancing in regimental front was seen emerging from their woody cover at the left where they had evidently formed for a charge. On they cane, filling the air with yells and shouts. A young officer dressed in a blue velvet jacket, and riding a bay horse, led the column. Brandishing his sword, he shouted to his troops. "Come on boys, show your grit!" Riding up to within eight or ten rods of that part of our line occupied by the 112th Ill, while his ranks were swept by the steady aim of our troops, he demanded the colors of the regiment. Major Dow, whose blood was up, though admiring the dash and pluck of the young officer, replied with an emphatic expletive, "You can't have it." The next instant the Rebel commander, horse and rider, sank down under a shower of balls. His intrepidity deserved a better cause, and a better fate. The left of the line, under the charge of overwhelming numbers, now began to waver and give way. Gen. Sanders, who was endeavoring to rally the men—one account says he had just taken a musket from a dead soldier who had fired and was in the act of loading it a second time—when be received a mortal wound. He was borne from the field by his brave men and carried to the rear. The position by which by the indomitable steadiness of the Ohio, Kentucky, and Illinois troops had been so long held, against great odds, was lost. Our men fell back a quarter of a mile, taking possession of the next line of hills. This ended the contest for the day. The enemy threw forward his skirmishers, and irregular firing continued between them and our own until dark.

On the Clinton road a sharp skirmish was kept up with the enemy by the 27th and 11th Kentucky Cavalry until night, where we lost eight or ten men in killed and wounded. Our loss in the chief engagement was about 200, about half of whom, in wounded or prisoners, were left in the enemy's hands.

E.S.

KILLED AND WOUNDED IN THE FIGHT AT CAMPBELL'S STATION.

FORTY-FIFTH PENNSYLVANIA, KILLED, None. WOUNDED. P. Coyle, A, shoulder. Sgt. A. Bailey, B, hip. J. Sharbaugh, A, forearm. Jas. Lovee, H, knee. Sgt. G. H. Tremain, H, head. Henry Frink, B, mortally. J. Crider, E, mortally. Sgt. G. M. Hobaugh, C, thigh. Wm. Houseseal, A, forearm. A. H. Bryant, H, knee. H. Sermings, G, thigh.

FORTY-SIXTH NEW-YORK, WOUNDED. Sgt. 0. Charles, C, right side. T. Winkler, B, side, hand. J. Cooper, D, mortally. J. Eichner, K, right arm.

FIFTIETH PENNSYLVANIA. KILLED. Emanuel Faust, A. WOUNDED. Sgt. H. Gechler, H. A. Gift, E. M. McKeon, D. J.Bedford, K.

FIFTY-FIRST PENNSYLVANIA. KILLED—NONE. WOUNDED. Sergt. Frank Sterner, K, leg. William Robinson, C, foot. Sergt. Wm. Mellick, K, foot,

THIRTY-FIFTH MASSACHUSETTS. KILLED-NONE. WOUNDED. F. L Barnes, H, wrist. Corp. J. Anderson, B, hand. J. R. Thayer, F, ankle.

TWENTIETH MICHIGAN. KILLED. Lieut.-Col. J. Huntington Smith.

THIRTY-SIXTH MASSACHUSETTS. KILLED. Lieut. P. M. Holmes, B. H. E. Stevens, H. Sergt. S. R. Gallop, A. WOUNDED. Capt. Barker, A. Lieut. Fairbanks, K. W. H. Siner, A. L. B. Hall, D. G. Harwood, E. E. T. Hall, I. C. H. Wheeler, I. Corp. B. Chamberlain, K. G. W. Foster. Capt. Warriner, E. G. A. Sinclair, A. G. E. Plummer, D. Sergit Merrick, E. Corp. G. D. Davis, G. Corp E. W. Holton, G. Corp. F. Byron, K. S. Woodside.

TWENTY-NINTH MASSACHUSETTS. KILLED. Chas. H. Dwinnett, A. WOUNDED-NONE.

# THE BATTLES OF CHICKAMAUGA & CHATTANOOGA.

FROM THE MISSISSIPPI DISTRICT.

## THE BURNSIDE RELIEF EXPEDITION.—THE REPORTED DEATH OF BRECKINRIDGE CONFIRMED.—THE RETREAT OF BRAGG.—A SEVERE FIGHT AND HEAVY LOSS AT RINGGOLD.—HEROIC BRAVERY AND SUCCESS OF OUR TROOPS.—LIST OF OUR CASUALTIES.—SPLENDID RESULTS OF THE LATE VICTORIES—LARGE CAPTURES OF ARMS AND PRISONERS.—PROSPECTS OF A NEW CAMPAIGN.—THE ENEMY THOROUGHLY ROUTED AND DEMORALIZED.

Cincinnati, Saturday, Dec. 5, 1863.

The Gazette has the following dispatch:

Chattanooga, Friday, Dec. 4, 1863.—Everything is quiet along the entire line.—Our casualties in the late battle were 4,500. —We captured 6,450 prisoners, and 46 guns.

## THE RETREAT OF BRAGG—THE ROUT AND THE PURSUIT—ARTILLERY AND RESOURCES TAKEN—A SEVERE FIGHT AND HEAVY LOSS AT RINGGOLD.

From our special correspondent. Battlefield Ringgold, Ga., Nov. 27, 1863

BRAXTON BRAGG.

After the shattered and panic-stricken forces of Bragg were driven from Missionary Ridge, Sherman of the 15th Army Corps was ordered to follow up and harass him on the left, with a portion of the 11th, 15th, and 14th Corps, and Hooker to follow him on the Woodberry and Ringgold dirt road, while Gen. Palmer of the 14th Army Corps was to make for his center. Sherman started about 1 o'clock p. m. of the 25th, and on reaching Chickamauga Creek he found the bridge had been burned and the enemy making fast time toward Ringgold and Dalton. Sherman dispatched immediately to Gen. Grant for instructions as to the best mode of procedure, and it was quickly determined to throw a pontoon across the creek and follow Bragg. This caused considerable delay. Gen. Jeff. C. Davis of Gen. Palmer's Division was in the advance of the 11th and 15th Corps, and succeeded in saving a large quantity of corn, rice meal and other commissary stores at Chickamauga Station. The Rebels set fire to everything in their rear but our advance was in such close proximity to their rear that we saved a good deal of property which might have otherwise been destroyed. There must have been at least 75,000 bushels of corn and meal preserved. About dark Gen. John Beatty and Col. Dan McCook's Brigade of Davis's Division came upon a large body of the enemy's cavalry and infantry, drawn up in line of battle, when both our brigades were brought into line and advanced on the enemy, who was covered by a thick belt of woods, while our forces had to advance through an open field. This lasted an hour and a half. We in the mean time drove the enemy. Seeing that there was no other alternative, the Rebels set fire to their wagons and ingloriously fled toward Graysville. The wagons set on fire were engaging and harassing the enemy's rear, Gen. Palmer on the center pushed on at his best speed filled with ammunition, but our men succeeded in putting out

BATTLE OF CHATTANOOGA

FAC-SIMILE PRINT BY L. PRANG & CO.

the fire out before any damage was done. While we were engaging and harassing the enemy's rear, Gen. Parker on the center pushed on at his best speed with Johnson's and Baird's divisions of his corps, and succeeded in reaching Graysville as the enemy were setting the bridge on fire. They had it fired in four places as Palmer came up with Gen. Johnson's division. Then he compelled the very men who set the bridge on fire to extinguish the flames. A few miles above this Gen. Johnson captured four 12-pound Napoleon guns of English manufacture, together with horses, drivers, caissons, and ammunition, beside 250 prisoners. The Rebels threw two of their guns and caissons into the Chickamauga, all of which will be recovered by us. Meantime Gen. Davis's division came up—not, however, before Johnson had gained the point. At the capture of those guns the Regular brigade, Gen. King's, displayed great bravery and coolness. This morning, at 6 o'clock, Palmer ordered Johnson to follow the Rebels to Ringgold or the mountains, and fight them wherever found. Bragg, with the panic-stricken fragments of his army, was making his best time into Georgia, Dalton being the point he desired to reach. He had already gained a considerable start. Hooker's forces took the main road to Ringgold, while Sherman took a parallel road, and Thomas another route still. Hooker having the shortest route, reached Ringgold first, where he found the enemy posted in a very strong position in the town. After an hour's hard fighting he succeeded in dislodging them, when they took up another position still stronger, on the side of the mountain, in the rear of the town. The position, very much resembled Missionary Ridge, only it was a stronger one. Six pieces of artillery having been captured, they had but two left. With these they opened fire on the village. Hooker determined to dislodge them by assault. The divisions of Geary and Osterhaus were selected for this purpose. Gen. C. R. Woods, of Osterhaus's Division, was directed to ascend by the left flank, and Col. Creighton, commanding a brigade of Geary's division by the left flank-both to gain a position in the rear of the enemy higher up. The enemy were in superior force, and our advancing columns were assailed with great fierceness, and twice repulsed. The fighting was of the most desperate description on both sides. Rallying for the third time, and climbing the steep under a most galling fire, our forces reached the summit and planted there their colors. It was when making this last most desperate charge that the gallant Creighton fell mortally wounded. The enemy fled, their object being to burn two railroad bridges on their rear near by Williamson's brigade, of Osterhaus' division, closely pursued and prevented the destruction of the bridges. The driving of the enemy from this strong position cost dearly. Our loss in this single operation will not be less than 500, and will probably reach 800. Ireland's (N. Y.) brigade particularly distinguished itself, capturing three stand of colors.

The following is the list of casualties among the officers:

FIRST BRIGADE, GEARY'S DIVISION, TWELFTH ARMY CORPS.

Col. V. R. Creighton, of the 7th Ohio, commanding brigade, killed. Lit.-Col. 0. J. Crane, 7th Ohio, killed. Lieut. Joseph Currin, 7th Ohio, killed. Adjutant Morris Baxter, 7th Ohio, wounded mortally. Capt. McClellan, 7th Ohio, wounded mortally. Lieut. C. Nesper, 7th Ohio, wounded mortally. Lieut. Jones, 7th Ohio, wounded mortally. Lieut. Brown, 7th Ohio, wounded mortally, amputation of both legs. Lieut. Lockwood, 7th Ohio, wounded severely. Lieut. Bohn, 7th Ohio, wounded severely. Lieut. McKay, Inspector-General of Brigade, wounded severely In both legs. Lieut. Spencer, 7th Ohio, wounded slightly.

Out of the thirteen officers of the above regiment, only one, Capt. Cruger, escaped, and he had his hat shot off and his coat badly riddled.

BATTLE OF CHATTANOOGA.

SIXTY-SIXTH OHIO.

Lieut. Harry Davis, Co. H, killed.

TWENTY-EIGHTH PENNSYLVANIA.

Lieut. Kaylor, Co. F, wounded seriously. Capt. Wade, wounded slightly. Adjutant Sam. Goodman, wounded slightly.

ONE-HUNDRED-AND-FORTY-SEVENTH PENNSYLVANIA

Capt. Davis, wounded mortally. Lieut. Parks, wounded severely. Total number of officers in First Brigade killed and wounded-18.

ONE-HUNDRED-AND ELEVENTH PENNSYLVANIA

Lieut. Mead, slightly wounded.

TWENTY-NINTH PENNSYLVANIA.

Capt. Johnson, slightly wounded.

THIRD BRIGADE, SECOND DIVISION, TWELFTH ARMY CORPS, COL. DELAND COMMANDING.

Capt. Charles F. Green, A.A.A., leg amputated. Capt. Thomas Elliott, 60th N.Y., slightly wounded. Lieut. McKinstry, 140th N.Y., slightly wounded. Total number of killed and wounded in N.Y. Brigade—Killed, 8, Wounded, 45(?)

OSTERHAUS'S DIVISION OF SHERMAN'S CORPS, FIRST BRIGADE, BRIG.- GEN. C. R. WOODS COMMANDING. SEVENTY-SIXTH OHIO, MAJOR WARNER COMMANDING. Capt. Ira P. French, 76th Ohio, killed. Lieut. John P. Miller, 76th Ohio, killed. Lieut. S. B. Wall, 76th Ohio, mortally wounded. Lieut. John R. Lemert, 76th Ohio, mortally wounded. Lieut. John J. Mentger, 76th Ohio, severely wounded. Capt. Blackburn, 76th Ohio, slightly wounded. Total killed in 76th Ohio, 2 officers and 16 men.

TWELFTH MISSOURI. Col. Hugo Waryelin, arm amputated. Capt. Knecher, leg and arm amputated. Major L. T. Ledgegerber, severely wounded. Capt. Ledgegerber, killed. Adjutant F. Kesler, killed.

THIRTEENTH ILLINOIS. Lieut.-Col. Partridge, wounded in hand. Major D. R. Bushnell, killed. Capt. Blanchard, leg amputated. Capt. Beardsley, left arm amputated and eye shot out.

SEVENTEENTH MISSOURI. Lieut. Fisher, killed. There are two other officers of this regiment wounded, but we have not names up to writing.

THIRTY-FIRST MISSOURI. Capt. Wm. Judd, wounded severely in thigh.

BATTLE OF CHICKAMAUGA.

SECOND BRIGADE, FIRST DIVISION, FIFTEENTH ARMY CORPS. Col. Williamson, commanding. Capt. Ford, A. A. A. G., leg amputated. Lieut. Stimspon, A. D. C., slightly wounded. Lieut. Shields, Inspector-General, slightly wounded. The above officers belong to Col. Williamson's Staff.

NINTH IOWA. Lieut. Charles Lyman, lightly wounded.

FOURTH IOWA. Lieut. Thomas Kramer, killed.

TWENTY-SIXTH IOWA. Capt. J. D. Steele, seriously wounded. Lieut. W. Nichols, slightly wounded. Lieut. N. D. Hubbard, slightly wounded.

THIRTEENTH IOWA. Lieut. Ethan Milliken, slightly wounded.

TWENTY-FIFTH IOWA. Lieut.-Col. Palmer, slightly wounded. Adjutant S. W. Snow, seriously wounded. Lieut. John A. Young, slightly wounded. Lieut. M. R. Anderson, seriously wounded. Capt. J. B. Ritner, seriously wounded. Lieut. B. H. Crane, slightly wounded. Lieut. H. R. Dakes, slightly wounded.

This brigade gloriously distinguished itself in driving the Rebels from the ledge on the far side of the mountain. Later in the day Gen. Sherman formed a junction with Hooker at Ringgold. Their future operations will have reference to the railroad at the nearest point from Ringgold to prevent the junction of Longstreet with Bragg, who, it is probable, will not be further pursued. C. D. BRIGHAM.

## THE GREAT VICTORY—THE SPLENDID RESULTS—OTHER GREAT RESULTS TO FOLLOW—THE ENEMY UTTERLY DISGUSTED AND DEMORALIZED—WHAT YET MAY BE DONE.

From Our Special Correspondent. CHATTANOOGA, Nov. 26, 1863.

If ever Chattanooga was in any sense besieged, the siege has been thoroughly raised by the events of the last three days. So much has been gained with so little loss, that it is difficult to realize fully the real state of the case. The fact is, Bragg was whipped from the start. The plan of operations contained so many inevitable combinations that he could not prevent being whipped one way or another. It was like a stove that would stand on one leg while it had three good ones. Had we gained by hard fighting and the loss of thousands of lives what has been secured by strategy, with a loss perfectly insignificant, when compared with the results, it would have been considered a splendid victory—and so it would have been.

It was only five days ago that Bragg sent by flag of truce to Gen. Grant to send the non-combatants out of Chattanooga, for he was going to shell the place. He to-day is a fugitive, his army demoralized, fleeing for [his] very life, with no prospect of gaining a position having anything like the advantages for defensive as well as offensive operations as the one he has been driven from almost by a frown.

Gen. Brown, who brought Bragg's ridiculous message, made hold to say that he was ready and willing to stake the fate of the Confederacy on a single battle at Chattanooga, and in saying this he believed he spoke the sentiment of Bragg's army, and of the South generally. The battle has taken place, and it is presumed that Gen. Brown has no doubts about the result. Will he accept it as deciding the fate the Confederacy?

The Rebel newspapers have for the last six weeks spoken of the forthcoming battle at Chattanooga, which they were to bring on, as the "final struggle" because it would decide the question of repossessing Tennessee and Kentucky, without which States the Confederacy could not live. Will they confess the full force of the result?

While far more has been accomplished than we had any reason to expect, with a loss so small that in comparison it is almost ridiculous, the results are just what the original plan contemplated. Nor has the plan yet culminated. Before this can get into print, the country will have additional fruits of that plan to rejoice over.

Bragg has been disposed of finally, if the Rebellion has not received the killing blow. In conversation to-day with prisoners taken, I heard many expressions of disgust toward him from officers as well as privates. They said that such a thing as an attempt to assault Missionary Ridge was not dreamed of by them. That we should have carried the ridge they fully admit completely confounded them. A Mississippian said to me that the taking of Lookout broke the spirit of the army. While the daring of our men in making the assault will stand without a parallel, I think there is an element in that splendid achievement to be attributed to the fact that the rebels had no heart to make the defense they might have made. I can attribute our small loss and, the precipitate flight of the enemy to nothing else.

The capture of from sixty to eighty pieces of artillery, the putting to flight of the entire Rebel army, the destruction of a vast amount of property, the taking of from three to five thousand prisoners, was effected in the space of less than one hour, and with the loss of less than five hundred men in killed and wounded.

Those who to-day visited Missionary ridge were astounded with these facts. Had 5,000 lives been the forfeit it would have been considered cheap, to say nothing of the other advantages won. The Rebel commanders, from Bragg down, did not doubt the position was by nature as nearly impregnable as it could be. While we give all credit to the heroism of our soldiers, is there not a good deal to be attributed to the loss of heart by the Rebel army? And may we not conclude that the time has come when we may count on the weakness of a broken spirit—a sure presage of the end.

I have been struck with another fact to-day. With scarcely an exception the Rebel prisoners were not down cast, while many of them actually rejoiced. They are from all parts of the South, and this is the common sentiment among them. Letters were found written by husbands to their wives breathing nothing but a disgusted and discouraged feeling in regard to the war, ever before have I seen prisoners captured so easily. Many of them ore than half deserted. This is not true chiefly of conscripts, but of the oldest enlisted men, and some of this sort are from South Carolina. There is something beside chance in all this. I think these things mean a great deal.

Bragg having been beaten and put to flight, I presume the country, in case he is not caught or his army utterly demolished, and more especially if this is done, will expect Grant to push on till he finds another army to fight. Few know what such an idea contemplates—how much such an expectation requires of a general. Napoleon fell because he went to Moscow. The further Grant advances the further will he be from his base, which for the present must be Louisville, or some point not much nearer. Had Chattanooga, which must be his depot a six month's supply, the case would be different. Here we come back to the cause of the wretched generalship immediately succeeding the battle of Chickamauga. There are physical impossibilities, and some of the things that will be expected of Gen. Grant will doubtless be found to be among them. The General who has done so much will do all he can. This is worth bearing in mind.

## WHERE IS LONGSTREET?—HIS COMMUNICATIONS CUT OFF—THE PURSUIT OF BRAGG CANNOT BE LONG FOLLOWED UP—HE IS HELPLESS AND HARMLESS—CONCENTRATION FOR ANOTHER GREAT BLOW—THE SPOILS OF BATTLE.

From Our Special Correspondent. Chattanooga, Nov. 27, 1863.

Where is Longstreet, and what about him? This is the question that comes up, now that Bragg has been disposed of. Prisoners say that Bragg sent for Longstreet to hurry to his support, several days ago, and that when Bragg commenced running he was expecting Longstreet to come up in two or three days. To-day the only road practicable for him to bring anything beside men will be in our hands; to-day Longstreet has no transportation, and depends on the railroads. It is certain, therefore, that he can escape only by back routes, and with only what his men can carry. Bragg maneuvering for a junction and a stand at or near Dalton, between 30 and 40 miles distant, at the junction of the Chattanooga with the Knoxville and Atlanta Railroad. He will probably succeed in gathering the fragments of his army there.

JAMES LONGSTREET.

The pursuit of Bragg will not continue far, solely on the ground of supplies and transportation. It is absolutely impossible. Bragg owes the escape of the fragments of it his army solely to the fact that there is not forage enough in the country to feed our cavalry, which was not ordered to pursue on that account. It may be difficult for the distant reader to understand this; and some may be disposed to be dissatisfied because the pursuit is not kept up, when the fact is, it is a stroke of generalship not to pursue, under circumstances such as now surround us. Besides, Bragg is thoroughly smashed, and there is very little game left in him or his army. A blow has been struck, the moral effect of which will be tremendous on the South. The next blow will follow in good time and in the right place. The arm that dealt this has undiminished strength.

Without anybody to annoy their flanks, Grant and Thomas will now be free to turn their attention to making this the depot for future operations, which will be postponed not a day longer than is practicable to resume them. Tennessee is now permanently free from the Rebels, for what force there may have been opposed to Barnside [sic] will make good their exit soon or not at all.

Among the immediate consequences of this great achievement will be practically a large increase of Grant's force. I presume Burnside will soon effect a junction, while the large force heretofore protecting our right flank having been in a great measure relieved, no small part of it will probably be added to the main body. This concentration is not among the least considerable results of the victory. It renders available another army of no mean proportions with which to deal the next blow.

Prisoners continue to come in hourly. They all tell the same story. Many of them openly curse Bragg, and say that his army has the same feeling.

The number of pieces of artillery captured, though not as large as has been reported, is yet larger than was first supposed. To-day the inventory is forty pieces, including a full battery of the celebrated Washington Artillery of New-Orleans. Of small-arms there will be a very large number—somewhere from six to ten thousand—beside considerable other property, including a large number of mules. Of the enemy's loss in killed and wounded we have no trustworthy data. In the nature of the case it must have been more than ours. Added to the prisoners already in our hands, this makes Bragg's total loss, up to the present time, not much under 10,000. This will be increased, for Sherman, Hooker, and a part of Thomas's forces are harassing Bragg's retreat, killing and capturing continually, beside taking and destroying his trains. Our loss in prisoners is a mere nothing. The 11th Corps had a few men captured out of a New-Jersey regiment day before yesterday. Beyond this I do not hear of a dozen captures. C. D. Brigham.

## THE BURNSIDE RELIEF EXPEDITION—REPORTED DEATH OF BRECKINRIDGE CONFIRMED.

Cincinnati, Saturday, Dec. 6, 1863. The Commercial has the following dispatch: CHATTANOOGA, Friday, Dec. 4,1863.

Capt. W. W. Mann, 41st Ohio, wounded on he 23d, while gallantly driving the Rebels from Orchard Knob, died on Wednesday night.

The expedition to relieve Burnside is under Sherman. It has no doubt arrived.

A heavy force here and on Lookout Mountain is preparing for the Winter defense of this place. The work on the railroad to Bridgeport is progressing. The bridge on Running Water is going up rapidly, and when completed the road will be in a fine condition. Bridge-builders from the North have arrived.

Breckinridge's death is confirmed.

The Rebels in the hospital are doing well. There are a few cases of small pox. They are visited daily by Secesh women.

About two hundred Union wounded have died in the hospital.

# THE SIEGE OF KNOXVILLE.

## THE ATTACK ON FORT SANDERS—DESPERATE STRUGGLE BY LONGSTREET—THRILLING DETAILS OF THE FIGHTING—HEROIC COURAGE OF OUR TROOPS—COMPLETE FAILURE OF THE ATTACK—THE CITY OF KNOXVILLE IS SAVED.

Special Dispatch to the Chicago Tribune. Cincinnati, Dec. 3, 1863.

Captain W. Anderson, Assistant Adjutant-General, Department of the Ohio, has received the following official dispatch:

KNOXVILLE, Nov. 30, Via Cumberland Gap, Dec. 2d, 1863.

The enemy attacked us early this morning in force, but we repulsed them with considerable loss. All is well. A. E Burnside, Major General.

Special Dispatch to the Chicago Tribune. KNOXVILLE, Nov. 30, 1863.

The great rebel blow, anxiously anticipated so long, was struck yesterday morning. Reinforced by the troops of Sam Jones, Jackson and Williams, Longstreet sought to annihilate the Army of the Ohio by coup de guerre. He selected seven picked regiments.

Skirmishing commenced on Sunday night at ten o'clock, and continued sharply until near daylight of Monday on our left front before Fort Sanders, commanded by Gen. Ferrero and defended by the 79th New York, Benjamin's 3d U. S. Artillery, and Buckley's Rhode Island Battery.

Our pickets were driven in and the enemy had possessed themselves of some rifle-pits, but the Massachusetts boys drove them back, when suddenly the Rebel storming party, led by the 16th and 17th Georgia and 13th Mississippi, under cover of our own retreating men, came to the assault.

They approached to within one hundred yards of the fort unharmed. Then commenced a series of desperate and daring attacks, stubborn resistance, death, carnage, and horror scarcely equaled during the war. These men were the veterans of the Potomac—the flower of Longstreet's army—and confident of promised victory, plunged into the boiling hell of lead.

Wire had been stretched from stump to stump in front of the works by Capt. Poe. Over these the advancing enemy fell in confused heaps, with the killed and wounded around them.

Our artillerymen hurled shell by hand; forward, over the impediments, came the doomed Rebels! Hot, and hotter, became the battle, until the ground over which they passed was carpeted with the slain. The ditch was piled with dead, wounded, and dying.

Not one on their side faltered—not a score of the gallant stormers escaped. The sun, rising, looked down through the cold mist and chill frost of that November morning upon the remains of an army.

ASSAULT ON FORT SANDERS.

One thousand killed, wounded, and prisoners, was the cost of the assault of Fort Sanders. Nobly has it sustained the reputation of its namesake and revenged his fall! Among the killed is Col. Girarde of the 13th Massachusetts. Lieut.-Col. O'Brien, the brother of Mrs. Brownlow, is a prisoner.

Gen. Burnside offered them an armistice from 10 a. m. to 5 p. m., to remove their wounded and bury their dead. It was accepted. The rebel officers and prisoners express astonishment at the strength of our works and the valor of our men.

Our loss will lot reach eighty, all told. Over fifty of these are the men of the 27th Kentucky, captured on the south of the river.

Whether Longstreet is satisfied with the impregnability of Knoxville, we know not, but await his next movement with confidence.

Besides 250 prisoners, we have three battle flags. One of them was planted on our works at one time.

LATER—The twelve days of Longstreet before Knoxville, threatening assault and siege, had caused a scarcity of forage, gave us considerable labor to fortify our position, and temporarily suspended our communications and destroyed much property, chiefly Rebel. There has been some lose of men by the casualties of war, but no panic retreat, starvation or actual investment has occurred thus far. The siege is another Rebel failure.

The mettle of the men of both sides has been tested, and our boys found to have no awe of Longstreet's veterans.

Daily skirmishing has been spirited, and on several occasions very severe, with lively shelling on both sides.

Our troops have behaved splendidly throughout. Our loss will not exceed 300 in all, many of whom are slightly wounded and returning to duty.

We can ill afford the loss of the gallant Sanders, who is universally regretted.

Our principal fear now is that the Rebels will escape without punishment for their impudence. Our army is in excellent spirits and improved health.

## A QUIET NIGHT—PREPARATIONS FOR DEFENSE—MOVEMENTS OF THE ENEMY—KNOXVILLE BESIEGED—THE ENEMY BALKED—BURNSIDE FELL BACK FROM LONDON TO HELP GRANT—NATURE OF KNOXVILLE DEFENSES—TIMIDITY OF NON- COMBATANTS—DESIGNS AND POSITION OF THE ENEMY

From Our Special Correspondent. Knoxville, Nov 19, 1863.

The night passed quietly. There was no demonstration of the enemy. The sharp crack of the skirmisher's rifles and the occasional crash of falling trees at times awaked their echoes on the still midnight air. The enemy were evidently at work, making the best use of their time.

Within our own lines, along every part fronting the enemy, parties were busy with men demolishing houses and felling trees which obstructed the view, or interfered with the working and range of our guns. Fatigue parties around the entire lines were busy throwing up breastworks, and digging rifle-pits, and strengthening our position for the expected morning attack. The soldiers, poor fellows, have had little rest, day or night for nearly ten days past, and it is matter of surprise that human nature can endure so much of watching, exposure and hard work. The morning was smoky, so that little could be seen at daylight, but at sunrise a line of earthworks was discovered across a plowed field to the left of the Kingston road, within a thousand yards of our position. The enemy's skirmishers had crept up to a wooded ravine running transversely across our western front, directly at the foot of the long slope, at the top of which stand our entrenchments. They also got possession of a brick house (Mr. Tames Armstrong's), from which they attacked our pickets, shooting one of our men from the scuttle of the roof. Two or three well-directed shells ventilated the house and drove them out.

Here is a new condition of affairs. Instead of being the attacking party, as almost always has been the case heretofore, we are now acting wholly on the defensive, occupying a besieged town, behind our hastily constructed works, and the Rebels are digging rifle-pits and trenches to get at us. I observe, however that they practice something of that prudence in approaching a fortified position which has sometimes drawn down the derision of the unthinking upon our own men. No troops, however brave, care to attack a place where the odds are so much against them, and where it is almost certain death to venture. Our troops like the change, and seem to think it only fair that they should, once in a while, take their turn behind the rifle-pits.

## PLANS OF THE ENEMY BALKED.

One of our orderlies who fell into the hands of the Rebels, and who afterward escaped, heard the officers and soldiers in Longstreet's Corps express their belief that he would retreat upon Cumberland Gap without stopping. Had we done so, or made the attempt, it would have been fatal to the whole command. The retreat could never have been conducted a hundred miles across these mountain roads and gorges without exposing the entire line to annoyances by the enemy which would have demoralized it, subjected it to panic, stampede, and capture. This may be truthfully asserted, whatever may happen to us here. Gen. Burnside foreseeing this, and intending to serve a far higher and nobler purpose with his command than running to save it, safely retired his forces within this place, determined to do his share in fighting the great battle of the war by occupying Longstreet's veteran corps as long as possible, while Grant was moving upon the works of Gen. Bragg at Chattanooga. It was for this purpose that he fell back from Loudon, instead of contesting the advance of the enemy. Should affairs go well with Gen. Thomas, the country will have little cause of regret for whatever may happen to this immediate command. We are not only fighting here the best drilled troops in the Confederacy, but are, at the same time, holding East Tennessee. We hope to hold our position.

## HERCULEAN LABORS PERFORMED.

Within the last 24 hours an almost incredible amount of labor has been performed upon the defenses of Knoxville. Lines of rifle-pits crown the whole range of hills around, and to the right and left of the town. The position itself is as strong almost as nature could have made it for sustaining an assault or maintaining a siege.

A large portion of the north side of the town, along which runs the railroad track, has been flooded by damming up two important streams, known as "First" and "Second" Creeks, on the map of the place. These creeks empty into Holston, one toward the eastern, and the other at the western division of the town. The water has been turned back until these streams proper are impassable except upon bridges—which have been destroyed —while in the valley along which they run, at the very base of the hill, which are crowned by our batteries and rifle-pits, the land is flooded to several feet in depth. No line of troops can advance unbroken in the face of this obstacle. Thus our northern front, from the center well to the right, is pretty well protected. From the bed of First Creek, which runs north and south through the place, dividing East from West Knoxville, Temperance Hill, rises to an altitude of almost 125 feet, and this ridge continues east in gradually ascending slopes far about a mile to Mayberry Hill, having an average width of a quarter of a mile. There are several strong earth works and batteries on Temperance Hill, capable of commanding the plain in front for three quarters of a mile. Rifle pits have been run entirely around this line of hills, the eastern portion leaving three lines, one in the rear of the other, so that if driven from the first, they can retire to the second and third line of defense. The south and south-east sides are protected by the river on which our lines rest, both on the left and right.

Anyone who visits these works, and sees what has been accomplished in so short a time, will be struck with admiration for the energy as well as the genius which has planned and consummated them. Captain Poe of the Regular Army, and late Colonel of the 20th Michigan, Chief the Engineer Corps, has cooperated with the Commanding General in laying out and executing these important works of defense in a manner which should secure for him the gratitude of his country. Gen. M. D. Manson, who has the command of the right wing of the defense, has also been ably assisted by Gen. Haskell, who has collected and organized about two thousand loyal Tennesseans, raw troops, who have been lately enlisted. These have been placed in a position to render valuable assistance against the enemy, when the grand assault is made. While the attack was imminent, and before there had been time to complete the rifle pits, he caused log breastworks to be constructed from the felled trees which afford excellent protection to rifle men, The entire front of the right line is protected by a chevauz de frise of pikes, the shafts of which are strongly inserted in the parapet at an angle of 45 degrees, and freely secured by telegraph wire. These pikes were found here when we took possession. Among many other articles intended for the defense of the place from the Union army, earthworks, with strong traverses cover our batteries at every important place with magazines well covered from the enemy's guns.

One part of tile town, directly fronting the railroad track, falls away in an abrupt descent of 50 feet at an angle of 45 degrees. This bluff is crowned by rifle-pits along the crest, with logs for the protection of the mens' heads. The left of the hill, to where it slopes more gradually toward the level of the railroad track, is strongly protected by batteries of cotton bales and earth. Here is Edward's fine battery of rifled guns belonging to Col. Siegfrieds's brigade. To the right of Gay street, which runs from the river north to the railroad, a strong battery also of cotton bales and earth is established. The street is barricaded by wagons and bales of cotton. Rifle-pits also extend right and left across a narrow plateau ending at First Creek. Today, at noon, this last-named battery opened upon a party who were noticed on the opposite hill planting some guns in position, and obliged them to withdraw, The Rebels, however, first fired three or four shots into the town, at the battery, which fell doing no damage, though they produced some slight "stir." One or two of these missiles passed over the roof of the house where your correspondent was engaged in chronicling events, and suggested the query in his man whether it was a safe place for permanent board.

These half-dozen shots are all that have thus far been fired into the town. I constantly hear it asked by citizens, will General Longstreet get up a general bombardment of the town, without first giving timely notice and permitting non-combatants (your correspondent is among them), with the women and children—I like their society—to withdraw. I reply, certainly not. Is not General Longstreet an officer of the Regular Army, and will he do so irregular a thing? Is he not a gentleman, a soldier, and, for aught I know, a Christian, and will he slaughter innocent women and children without giving them due notice? Certainly not. Besides, are there not hundreds of the best friends the Southern Confederacy ever had still living in the town, and praying for his success? Thus I endeavor to console the people, and keep them quiet, of course feeling perfectly calm myself, and having not the slightest apprehension of danger. Whether these assurances have any effect or not, I observe much more quiet in the town than could have been expected.

Gen. Burnside frequently visits all parts of the line in person to insure instantaneous communication between the extremes of the lines and his own headquarters, a telegraph wire has been stretched through the town from Fort Sanders on Tape Hill, the west front, to Temperance and Mayberry Hills, connecting with headquarters. The same line connects with Col. Cameron's position, crossing the pontoon bridge. The signal flag stations are also located on the most prominent points, having a view of the whole field, and transmitting from one point to the other prompt intelligence of the enemy's movements.

The enemy gradually advanced his skirmishers around toward the center of our position, taking advantage of a belt of woods, on higher ground than that occupied by ours, and crept up to thin grove of oak and pine skirting the woods. Edward's battery flied an occasional shot at the party observed on an opposite hill engaged in building earth works for a battery.

## WHAT THE ENEMY IS DOING—HIS POSITIONS.

While we have a Strong position—strong by nature, and strengthened by the best engineering skill—the enemy has also great advantages for attack; and, aside from the question of food for men and animals, he no doubt regards the capture of the place as only a work of time. Last, in any untoward event, our brave army and its commander should be improperly criticized, I ought to describe the situation more fully. The enemy's right at present rests on the river, his forces finding ample protection among the hills and valleys through which runs the Kingston road toward the south-west, The whole country is hilly. The direction of the hills is generally at right angles to the river, obliging us to hold these clear to the bank of the stream, lest the enemy should come up under its cover to turn our flank. If possible, I have no doubt he will cross below and endeavor to occupy a high range of hills which we could not conveniently take possession of. Toward their left, the hills, or a part of them, are high, and all have a growth, more or less dense, of timber, which, to a great degree, conceal their movements from observation. Occasionally we obtain glimpses through the partial openings of bodice of cavalry passing. The enemy to-day have evidently been looking out favorable positions for locating batteries. In an air-line of an average distance of a mile from Edward's Battery, Sigfried's command, is a line of hills gradually rising from the enemy's left to a high point north-west by west of the town. That point is higher than the bluff on which the last-named battery is located. A plateau intervenes occupied by farms, crossed by fence enclosures in different directions, and through which run the Clinton Railroad, the country road to the same place, and that to Taezwell [sic]. Still back of this high land is a country by-road on which we see their wagons and artillery passing. This road intersects the Taezwell[sic] road at a distance of say two miles from the north side of the town. From about our center, nearly to the extreme right, the country is more level and open, with only scattering clumps of pines and scrub oaks. Here, then, are no positions favorable for batteries within a mile of ours. From our line the view is comparatively unobstructed. Still further round, the country becomes more hilly, and wooded hills and valleys extend to the Holston River, leaving one open space only on the extreme right, occupied by farms.

The 19th closed warm, with a hazy atmosphere.

## A CHARGE AND A CONFLAGRATION—SHELLING THE CITY—BRILLIANT SORTIE OF THE 17TH MICHIGAN—RAIN.

From our special correspondent. Knoxville, Nov. 20-Morning.

A smoky atmosphere obscures the fort and conceals the enemy's position and movements. There is an occasional shot from the pickets on either side, until 9 o'clock, when it cleared off, and the picket firing became quite general, particularly along the center, on the Clinton and Tazewell road. The skirmishers occupy nearly the same position as last evening at half a mile from our fortified line. The enemy's sharpshooters keep behind trees or fallen logs, and sometimes dig a hole in the ground from which they take aim at our pickets.

### A CHARGE AND A CONFLAGRATION.

About 10 o'clock a sudden discharge of musketry attracted attention at the center of our line. Our pickets advanced upon those of the enemy who had concealed themselves in a frame-house, and were annoying them. It was the residence of Mr. Braunan, brother of the President of Ocoll Bank. It was set on fire, and soon burned to the ground. Skirmishing continued with more or less activity until 5 p.m., when a there was a sudden cessation of firing. The Rebel pickets withdrew, as was supposed, for a night attack. Our pickets fell back, firing the buildings they had occupied during the day. They were a large brick dwelling and out-buildings located in the plain on the line occupied by our skirmishers, and two or three buildings in the scattered portion of the village beyond the railroad. It was intended as a measure of precaution, but they were prematurely fired. The buildings being in range of our batteries and rifle-pits, it may become necessary also to destroy a large portion of the railroad buildings and the houses contiguous to prevent them from being used as a cover for the enemy's sharp-shooters. A few moments before the conflagration, the enemy opened a battery near the front of our center, and fired four or five shots into the town. They were apparently aimed at the Cotton-bale Battery on Gay Street. The missiles, as they came whizzing into town, caused considerable panic, and for a few moments the impression prevailed among the citizens that the grand shelling had begun. The Gay street battery, as well as two others to the right and left, replied rapidly, their reports shaking the town. Spectators went skurrying [sic] for shelter to the neighboring buildings; teams skedaddled up Gay street, and citizens took to their cellars for protection. For some cause the Rebel batteries ceased firing, probably from a fear of hurting somebody in the town—ours followed suit—and there was a great calm. Meantime the heavens were illuminated by the lurid flames of the burning buildings, attracting a crowd of the mere venturesome to Summit Hill to witness the scene. The spectacle was grand and imposing to those who hod never witnessed a conflagration in New-York. These frequent illuminations seem so indicate that the entertainment coming off is to be got up without regard to expense. But seriously, nothing but the most urgent necessities of war, and such I suppose now exist, could justify the destruction of these homes. As covers for the Rebel sharpshooters (they are within easy rifle range of our batteries) they would be fatal to the occupation and working of our batterIes. The less, therefore, must be sacrificed to the greater.

Aside from this episode affairs soon became quiet. I omitted to mention that one of the shells fell in the yard of Gen. Burnside's headquarters, from which, however, he and his staff had moved during the day.

## BRILLIANT SORTIE OF THE SEVENTH MICHIGAN.

At 8 p.m. rapid cannonading was heard on our west front—Fort Sanders—which rousесd the town from its temporary repose. Now, it was supposed the expected night attack had began. The advance, it seems, was by our side, and not from that of the enemy. The Rebel pickets, during the day, had got into James Armstrong's house, just under the hill, and had very much annoyed our men. Gen. Ferrero accordingly ordered the 17th Michigan to make a sortie and drive them out. The work was handsomely accomplished, and the house set on fire. They then fell back; but as the light of the burning buildings burst forth it revealed the position of our men as they were deploying into the road, and the enemy swept their ranks by discharges of shell and solid shot. One Lieutenant was killed and three men wounded. Our batteries replied as fast as possible, covering our men as they retreated. The object was accomplished, though after sacrifice of valuable men, and the Michigan boys deserve much praise for the handsome manner in which they executed their task. The combined detonations of our own and the Rebel guns shook the town to it center, and citizens rushed into the streets to ascertain what was up. Some of the Rebel shells, passing over the fort on Tape Hill, fell in the streets of the town, causing some alarm. For a time the people watched the light of the blazing dwelling, but the batteries ceased firing, the flames gradually died out, and there was another great calm. The night passed without any other general alarm.

November 20,—During the latter part of the night rain began to fall heavily, and continued until 2 o'clock p. m. The country has been thoroughly drenched, and traveling on the roads impeded. The picket firing seems to be working around to the right. The evident intention of the enemy is to feel of our whole position before making the final attack. The rain, which is uncomfortable for both sides, must be particularly unfavorable for the Rebels, who have not yet got their guns in position or their works complete. Ours, luckily, were finished before the rain set in.

Nov. 21, Evening.—The afternoon has been, clear, with a bracing atmosphere—wind from the north-west. The enemy's pickets are about in the same position as yesterday. but the firing has not been active. Two or three have come in wounded. General Mausen gave the enemy two shots from his batteries on Temperance Hill, directed to the battery to the left oblique, but no response was elicited. There are rumors and reports of the enemy crossing a force over the Holston, below, with a view of attacking Cameron's position on Heith [Keith?] Hill.

## PROGRESS OF THE SIEGE.

From Our Special Correspondent. Knoxville Tenn., Nov. 22, 1863.

The siege of Knoxville is progressing, it is presumed, according to the most approved principles of warfare. Outside, the enemy keeps his skirmishers busy. He builds batteries, fells trees, constructs redoubts, and occasionally fires a shell into town, or at some one of our batteries. Inside, our forces lie in their rifle-pits or behind their well-constructed batteries, and watch the movements of the enemy. We are also indefatigable in strengthening the works of defense already constructed, and in extending them where they are needed. Every hour adds to the impregnability of the town against assault.

The morning dawned clear, with a bracing atmosphere, and the day has been one of the finest we have experienced for weeks. The roads are already fast drying, and traveling is getting passible. The enemy has been busy in the front of Summit Hill—which is his highest and most favorable position for artillery—and this morning reveals a large cleared space, two strong earthworks, and a line of rifle-pits around the crest of the hill, the whole at a distance of one mile in an air line. Their camp smoke has disappeared from the north side of the town, and a large camp is visible at the south-west, in the direction of which the chief attack was made on Tuesday, showing that they have their chief forces in that direction. To-day the respective pickets occupy about the same position as yesterday. There has been a brief truce between the enemy's pickets and those of the 11th New-Hampshire, and some pleasant raillery passing between them yesterday and to-day. "Have you got old [Parson] Brownlow in there?" "How comes on press?" "Have you had any mail lately?" "How are you in Vicksburg?" "Got plenty of mule meat on hand?" and such like queries, come from the Rebel side, and are answered according to the whim of the Union pickets. They wish to make me think they have captured one of our inward bound mails, which is quite likely; that they have captured "old Brownlow," which is unlikely, as he telegraphed "all safe" from Cumberland Ford a week ago; that they have captured his press, which we know has not started from Cincinnati, and various other things calculated to annoy us. The Rebels fired several shells at the battery on Temperance Hill about sunset, from the battery which I have already described—the range of fire being obliquely to then north front of the town—i.e, from north-west to south-east, nearly. One of the enemy's shells severely wounded a cavalry man who was standing in a group to the right of the battery. His lower jaw was carried away.

At 7 o'clock our battery opened upon enemy's position and fired some half a dozen rounds. There was no reply, and up to the present time, 8-1/2 p.m., everything remains quiet, There is a bright moonlight which is favorable to the operations of the enemy, and there is some expectation of a night attack on the town.

E.S.

KILLED AND WOUNDED AT THE SORTIE NIGHT OF NOV. 20.

Private Joseph Leonard, Co. F, 17th Mich., skull fractured by shell. Dead.

WOUNDED WHILE SKIRMISHING NOV 19TH, 20TH, AND 21ST.

2d Lieut. Alvin M. Reed. Co. D, 109 P.V., flesh wound, right hand. Wm. Cole, Co. I, 50th P.V., skull fractured. Corp. Phineas Bird, Co. C, 100 P.V., slt., frac. skull. Corp. Conrad Homan, Co. A, 29th Mass., flesh wound, right hand. Private. Jno. A. Connerly, Co. G, 100th P.V., right leg amputated above knee. Private Jno. W. Rodgers, Co. H, 100th Pennsylvania Volunteers, fracture of upper portion of arm; resection performed. Private Robert Burns, Co. G, 29th Massachusetts, flesh wound of shoulder and fracture of lower jaw; severe.

Monday, Nov. 22, 7-1/2 a.m.—Morning pleasant, but smoky on the hills. No sign of an attack. Everything in readiness and troops in good spirit.

## ARRIVAL OF COURIERS FROM CUMBERLAND GAP—CHEERING NEWS—A RECONNAISSANCE—FLAG RAISING—THE ENEMY TURNED BACK—ANOTHER FIRE—SORTIE BY THE 29TH MICHIGAN—ITS DISASTROUS FAILURE—LIST OF KILLED AND WOUNDED—DEATH OF GEN. SANDERS.

From our Special Correspondent. Knoxville, Nov. 23, 1863.

Having finished and enclosed to you a history of events up this morning, I begin a new chapter with the beginning of his week. The day has been still, Summer-like, and so warm in the sun as to be uncomfortable. Out of some eight or ten couriers sent from Cumberland Gap, two have arrived, bringing important and encouraging dispatches to Gen. Burnside. I understand the nature of the intelligence is that Gen. Grant "moved upon the enemy's works on the 20th," and that up to the 21st affairs were progressing favorably; that we have only to "hold on" here for a few days, when we shall receive succor. These announcements have given great encouragement to the officers and men of this command, not because we feel ourselves in any immediate danger, but because we all hope to see Bragg to retire back to Atlanta, and thus enable us to reopen the railroad via Chattanooga and Nashville, and forever put to rest the question as to the occupation of East Tennessee.

Gen. Shackleford, with a strong reconnoitering force, went a considerable distance up the Holston last evening in pursuit of a Rebel party reported to be in that quarter, but returned without finding any enemy. A bright lookout is kept in that direction.

## FLAG RAISING ON KEITH'S HIGHTS[sic].

Keith's Hights is a hill directly opposite the town on the south side of the Holston, rising at least 400 feet above the river level, and commanding not only the town but the country to the right, left, and to the rear, for the full range of our guns. This hill is reached from the river roads running within two hundred yards of its banks, at an average angle of say 30 degrees. From the rear it falls away in deep gorges, which it would be a half-hour's task for a strong-willed man to climb, even unopposed. Beyond is a line of hills somewhat lower, but still of sufficient hight to command the road and the valley, through which the enemy, in any assault, would have to pass. Between these is another round promontory, crowned by a redoubt along a ridge, which connects the two hills by a freshly-made road.

A few days ago these hights were covered with an almost impassable undergrowth and timber. To-day they are strongly fortified by a system of rifle-pits and re-doubts which furnish shelter for thousands of men, and for the most formidable batteries. The trees have been felled so as to form abatis on the river side and to the right, left and rear, a portion of the trees being used to form breastworks, which are banked up with earth. Col. Cameron, 65th Ill., having command of these defenses, has labored night and day to complete them in the most substantial manner. While occupying these hights, no army would be able, even if it should assault and enter the town, to remain in it for an hour. The enemy are fully posted as to the formidable nature of this position, and an assault for the capture of the place will, they know, necessitate, first of all, the taking of these hights, and the capture or isolation of the forces from those on the other side of the river. General Haskell, in whose command these important works are included, has personally supervised their planning and completion.

To-day, at noon, Col. Cameron having invited a number of officers to witness the ceremony, a handsome flag was thrown to the breeze, to float in triumph above the works. Gen. Haskell and staff, Col. Cameron and less brigade officers, with deputations of a company each from the 103d Indiana, 65th Illinois, and 45th Ohio, were present to greet the old flag with their cheers. General Haskell addressed the troops in a stirring speech, apologizing for the forced absence of Gen. Burnside, on account of pressing engagements elsewhere; complimented them for their efficient and valuable services in completing, in so short a time, this formidable line of defenses, and announced to them cheering intelligence from Chattanooga. Col. Cameron also addressed the men for a few moments, and pledged that himself and his command would be buried honorably beneath these works sooner than ever permit that flag to be hauled down. Three hearty cheers were given for the flag; three for General Burnside and Haskell, and three for Col. Cameron.

Before the ceremony was completed, a message came saying that the enemy were showing themselves in Col. Cameron's front. The Colonel immediately started with his men a quick march. It proved to be a reconnoisance[sic] of the enemy, who was stopped and driven back. They left one dead and a prisoner or two in our hands. During the last night the Rebels succeeded in digging a new line of rifle-pits somewhat nearer the works on Tape Hill, getting within five hundred yards of our gunners. Further to the right, they occupied their original position until dark, when a large force of their skirmishers suddenly advanced, driving our own in to the railroad. The buildings we occupied had been all prepared with combustibles ready to ignite, and under the order to fire them when compelled to fall back, the match was applied, and in a few moments there was

## ANOTHER CONFLAGRATION.

The Tennessee House, the large octagonal railroad building used for repairing, and formerly occupied by the Rebels as an arsenal, beside several houses outside the railroad, were fired. From 5 to 10 o'clock p. m. the heavens were aglow with red flame. During the Rebel charge rifle balls flew into the edge of the town quite profusely. A considerable number struck the walls of the Asylum Hospital, and several persons were said to have been hit who were standing about the premises.

Tuesday Morning, Nov. 24.—An advance was made by our pickets to the right of the railroad, and the enemy's sharpshooters, who had got into some of the buildings during the night, were driven out. The firing here was sharp for a few moments. The enemy's skirmishers had also crept up much closer to Gen. Ferrero's front during the last 24 hours, and it became necessary to make an effort to dislodge them. The attempt, I regret to say, failed, and we have lost, as near as can be ascertained, about 20 men in killed, wounded, and prisoners.

## SORTIE OF THE TWENTIETH MICHIGAN.

About 8 o'clock a.m., Gen. Ferrero, acting under orders, sent forward the 20th Michigan to charge the enemy's rifle-pits, and drive them out. The regiment was sustained by our batteries as long as it was safe to fire over the heads of the men. They went down the long slope, over the fallen trees, and through the debris in front, upon the double quick, attacking, driving out the Rebels from their pits, and occupying them for about half an hour, fighting hand to hand with the Rebels over the impalement. They met, however, a whole brigade, and being overpowered, sent back for reinforcements. Meantime, Adjt. Noble and Lieut. Galpin were killed, and Maj. Byington was badly wounded, beside a large number of men. The Major, probably seeing that the effort to hold the place was fruitless, ordered his men to retire. He was immediately made a prisoner.

Our men then fell back, bringing a portion of the wounded off the field. Only those who were badly hurt were made prisoners. Only some thirty were brought to the hospital, leaving twice that number killed, wounded, or prisoners in the enemy's hands. The affair is naturally discouraging to our men, and must be set down as the most unfortunate episode of the siege. Our dead are still lying within sight of our breast works, but cannot be recovered. I am told that the enemy invited our men to come after the wounded, and when they had advanced for the purpose of bringing them off the held, they were fired upon and compelled to withdraw. I can hardly credit such inhumanity, and only give the statement as I received it.

The Rebel rifle-pits are new so near our own that it is certain death to show one's head over our breastworks. An officer, who has just returned from Fort Sanders, says he could have thrown a stone from the fort into their nearest rifle-pits. This state of things cannot continue long.

### KILLED AND WOUNDED AT THE SORTIE OF 2ND MICHIGAN IN FRONT OF FORT SANDERS.

KILLED: Adjutant Noble, Lieutenant Chas. Galpin, Major Coruelius Irvington, supposed mortally wounded and captured.

WOUNDED: F. Holt, H, left arm G. Lee, H, rt. leg; J. Boss. A, left leg,; Sgt. F. P. Jones, C, rt. thigh; G.W. Couber, H, left leg, H. H. Percy, C, rt. thigh; A. Sears, K, wrist, Sgt. J. E. Martin, D, head; E. Vance, F, rt thigh; Corp. J. Pecker, H, ear, neck and back; N. H. Richards, F, toe, Lt. F. Zoeliver, B, left thigh; D. Palmer, E, rt. side; Sgt. S. Reinhart, L, rt hip, forearm and left forefinger; Corp. H. M. Casrow, B, left arm; J. CollIns, B, left arm and hip; J. McIntyre, G, rt. shoulder; Wm. Hills, D, left thigh.

There were no prisoners taken except the badly wounded.

LATEST, Nov. 25—The weather is clear and bracing. The enemy has made no assault or other large demonstration in front as yet. I, yesterday afternoon, counted five of his guns in position to the left of the Armstrong's, hence which I learn is Gen. McClaw's headquarters. A prisoner who has been in their hands for a few days came in to-day, and says the Rebels are waiting for reinforcements before they attack. He says he was treated kindly while in Rebel hands.

The Rebel pickets have possession of a high hill on the south side of the river, where we suspect it is their intention to place a battery. The hill commands Fort Sanders and the town. The truth is there are so many hills along the south side. of the river, it would take an immense force to occupy them all. There is no distress at present for food and forage in the town; and, outside of the hospitals, the health of the place is good.

It would be improper for me, in view of the danger of my letters falling into the hands of the enemy, to state what our expectations are as to getting reinforcements. It is only necessary to say that everybody is cheerful, and the troops in good spirits.

P. S. At 2 p.m. an engagement began on the south side of the river, Col. Cameron and Woodford being engaged. Do not know the result.

## DEATH OF GEN. SANDERS.

Gen Sanders received his wound upon the field about 3 o'clock p.m. The enemy had been repulsed several times, and his command was now staggering under a final charge of a whole brigade, led by one of the most, courageous of the Rebel officers. There was a deadly hand-to-hand fight. Sanders was leading his men, himself foremost in the contest. His conduct, no doubt, singled him out as the chief commander in the field, and he was made the target for the Rebel sharpshooters. He was struck by a minie ball, which passed through the cavity of the abdomen, lacerating the spleen and large intestines. He was removed to the rear, and conveyed immediately to town, where he was received under the care of Doctor Jackson, Medical Director of East Tennessee. The Doctor met him at the ambulance, and had him carefully removed on a litter to the Lamar House Hospital. After his wound had been examined, the General asked, "Tell me, Doctor, if my wound is mortal?" The Doctor replied, "Sanders it is a fearful wound, and mortal. I am very sorry to say it, my dear fellow, but the odds are against yet." The General calmly replied, "Well, I am not afraid to die; I have made up my mind upon that subject; I have done my duty, and have served my country well as I could."

His wound was dressed, and his pains relieved by morphia. His constitution never rallied, and he did not recover from the first shock and collapse. The remainder of his hours were spent as by a strong man dying. He lingered until 11 o'clock the next day, remaining perfectly conscious during the whole time. During the morning he explained certain symptoms to the doctor, and asked him what they meant. The doctor replied, "General you are dying." If that be so, he said, I would like to see a clergyman. The Rev. Mr. Heyden, Chaplain of the post, was sent for, who came immediately. Gen. Burnside, with some of his staff, Capt. Harris, a classmate, and several others were present. The minister addressed consoling words to the dying man, and afterward baptized him at his own request. "It was always the desire of my friends that I should be baptized." he said. The minister then joined in fervent prayer, Gen. Burnside and all present reverently kneeling beside the bed of the dying hero. It was a scene never to be forgotten. He shook hands with his chief, who stood tearfully over him, as if loth to witness the flight of the brave spirit.

In a few moments, and while preparations were making to administer to him the sacrament, his spirit took its flight. In the beautiful words of Dr. Jackson, "he went to sleep like a child." Thus passed away one of the bravest, yet one of the most unassuming men whom God has raised up to battle in the cause of good government.

## THE FUNERAL.

At 9 o'clock p.m. Major-Gens. Burnside and Park, with their staffs, Gens. Potter, Menses, Shackleford, Haskell, Carter, and White, with most of the regimental commanders (Sen. Ferrero being detained by the urgency of his presence at the front), assembled at the parlors of the Lamar House. The Rev. Mr. Hume of the Protestant Episcopal Church read a portion of the service for the Portal of the dead. The coffin was carried to an ambulance, and the procession moved, escorted by the military with reversed arms, the band of the 44th Ohio playing solemn dirges. The coffin was placed in a strong box and deposited in the church inclosure [sic] of the Presbyterian church.

The solemn march of the procession by moonlight and the mournful strains of the band as it moved to the place of burial was a scene the most impressive and affecting. Among the many friends who will mourn the sad but glorious death of the departed there will be few whose sorrow is more deep and abiding than that of the Commanding General.

Gen. N. P. Sanders was a native of Kentucky. He went to West Point from Mississippi; graduated in the class of '56; was appointed Captain of the 6th U. S. Cavalry; has been long attached to the army as a cavalry officer, (since the war); made the celebrated raid into East Tennessee as the John Bap. of Gen. Burnside; and has been one of the bravest and most active of Sen. B.'s associates. He had received his Brigadier's appointment but two or three weeks prior to his death. He was greatly beloved by the soldiers.

E.S.

Nov. 23 James Birnie, 50 Pa., right elbow. W. J. Coyle, B, 79 N.Y, right arm. P. McMillan, Col'd serv't. 5O Pa., left foot amputated. Wm. R. Crob, A, 2 Md., slight, chest. John Murphy, K, 48 Pa,, left hip.

Nov. 24 Corp A. Howask, en, H, 2lst Wis., left arm. Jonas Halderman, I, 48th Pa., left arm pit. Martin Tobin, C, 48th Pa., left foot. J. Weize, H, 48th Pa., groin. A. J. O'Dyer, G, 21St N. Y., right arm. Henry Cain, C, 21, hand slt'tly. Corp. F. Burpee, E, 21st Pa., right thigh. Chas. A. Giles, E, 11th N. H., breast, slightly. Jas. McGee, F, 21st Pa., right thigh. R. R. Fisk, B, 21st Mass.,head. Geo. W. Badger, D, 29th Mass., left ankle E. Terrell, E, 21st Pa., right side. Lt. Jacob Dobbin, K, 48th Pa., arm pit. M. Sinclair, C, 79th N. Y., face.

The list of officers is incomplete; there is no record made up.

E. S.

WOUNDED AT THE BATTLE OF KNOXVILLE.

THIRTY-SIXTH MASSACHUSETTS.

L. B. Hall, B. S. Woodside, K. Geo. W. Footer, K. Ezra J. Hill, I.

ONE-HUNDRED-AND-TWELFTH ILLINOIS.

Michael Nugent, C. A. J. Brade, B. A. C. Valentine, C. James Bice, C. D. P. Wandling, E. Sergt. A. B. Laferty, D. M. V. Cob, D. Jas. S. Rogers, D. Chas. H. W. Paine, D. Harry N. Mase, E. John Warters, A. Griffith Shaeck, C. Corp. Abner Norman, H J. W. Carfman, E. Corp. T. J. McClelland, G. P. I. Wintz, A. John Davis, C. Geo. Maconel, C. Corp. John Murray, K.

SEVENTEENTH MICHIGAN. Corp. Thos. MeKenna, A. Ozro Wentherby, K. Geo. F. Taylor, A.

EIGHTH MICHIGAN. Lt. Wilber Nelson, C. Manly White, B. Daniel Varnum, B. Eliphant Page, B. V. Mathem, E. Homer Manover, B. Lt. C. O. Frist, B. Geo. A. Hoyle, A. John Hill, K. Thos. Donnaly, H.

TWENTIETH MICHIGAN. Corp. Frank Phillips, H. A. Ludwig, H. J. A. Dell, H. J. Kennedy, II. Fred. Lehman, K.

FORTY-FIFTH OHIO. Sergt. W. P. Wallace, B. J. Stives, A. Wm. Manson, D. Sergt. John P. Noer, H. Wm. Smith, A. Corp. Hugh Tolan, D. Howard Line, G. Geo. Mayhall, A.

VARIOUS REGIMENTS. Capt. Alex. Armstrong, 115 Ind. Fred. Swint, I, 111 Ohio. J. A. Courtney, D, 100 P. V. E. P. Linvitte, C, 25 Ohio. Horace lnman, D, 2 Mich. Lt. W. H. Thornton, D, 1 Ky. Martin Conrad, E, 111, Ohio. Capt. Wm. T. Ward, B, 11 Ky. T. W. Miller, Bat., 23 Ind. Sergt. R. Scranton, 1, 11 Ky. Hiram Ferris, Bat., 5 R. I. Sergt Major W. H. Hale, F, 12 Ky. C. Teeple, F, 45 Pa. V. Geo. W. lrey, B, 1 Ky. Cav. Harden Stevenson, 1, 27 Ky. Corp. J. M. Patterson, G, 12 Ky. J. R. Irwin, K, 15 S. C., w'd In knee, and taken prisoner. J. J. Speck. C, 1 Ky. Sergt. T. G. Wells, E, 12 Ky. G. P. Clark, A, 12 Ky. Wm. O. Metcalf, E, 12 Ky. David B. Maloy, D, 27 Ky. Wesley Sims, E, 45 Pa. Sergt. Wm. C. King, D, 12 Ky.

KILLED. John Smith, B, 11 N. H. Dwight Ripley, K, 121 Me.

WOUNDED. NOV. 19, Lt. A. M. Reed, B, 100 Penn. Wm. Cole I, 50 Pa., skull, both legs fractured. Capt. F, B. Merrick, C, 35 Mo. Lt. Wm. S. Moore, 2 Mo., right arm, left side. McMulley, H, 2d Mo., right side.

Nov. 20 Corp. P. Bird, C, 100 Corp. 29 Pa., head. Conrad Homan, A, Mo., right hand. David Bowen, C, 2 Mo.,left hand. J. H. Frisby, 11, 2 Mo., left knee. John A. Adams, D, 2 Mo.

Nov. 21 John A. Crosby, G, 100 100 Pa.,right leg. John W. Rodgers, H, 100 Pa., shoulder Robt. Burns, G, 29 Mo., left arm.

Nov. 22 J. F. Wildermouth, H, 48 Pa., left hand. Henry Deibler, A, 50 Pa., left cheek.

# SCENES OF FORT SANDERS, KNOXVILLE, AND THE SURROUNDING AREA.

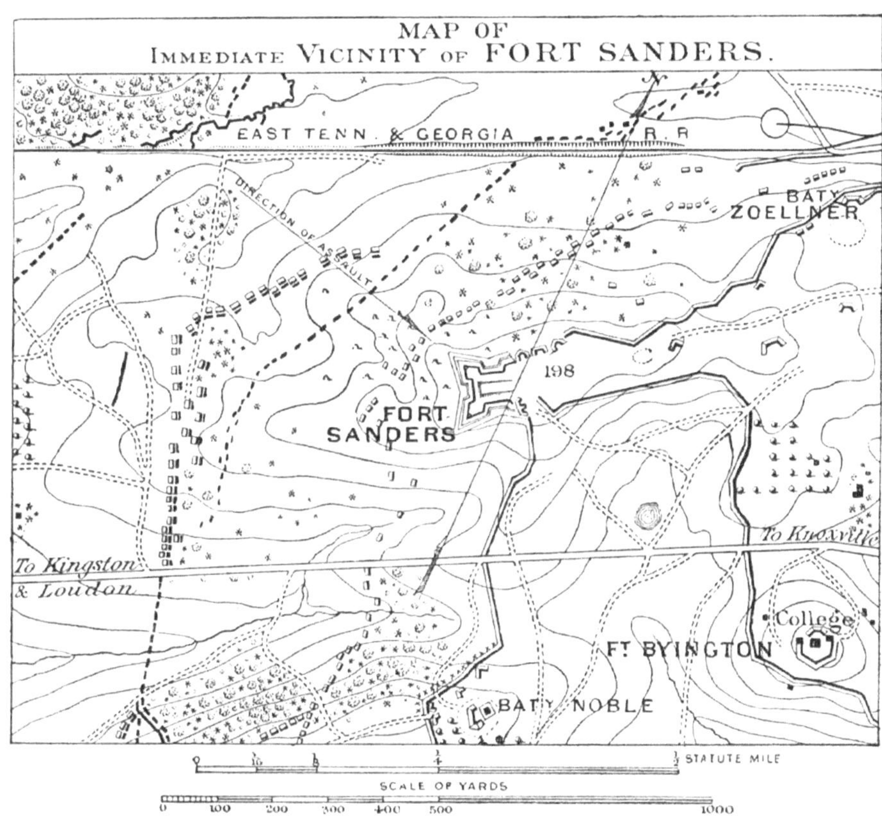

CONFEDERATE ASSAULT ON FORT SANDERS.

THE NORTH-WESTERN BASTION OF FORT SANDERS, VIEWED FROM THE NORTH. FROM A WAR-TIME PHOTOGRAPH.

THE NORTH-WESTERN BASTION OF FORT SANDERS, SHOWING THE GROUND OVER WHICH THE CONFEDERATES CHARGED. FROM A PHOTOGRAPH.

FORT STANLEY, KNOXVILLE. FROM A PHOTOGRAPH.

LONGSTREET'S ASSAULT ON FORT SANDERS.

HARPER'S WEEKLY
A JOURNAL OF CIVILIZATION

Vol. VII.—No. 356.] NEW YORK, SATURDAY, OCTOBER 24, 1863. [SINGLE COPIES SIX CENTS. $3.00 PER YEAR IN ADVANCE.

Entered according to Act of Congress, in the Year 1863, by Harper & Brothers, in the Clerk's Office of the District Court for the Southern District of New York.

THE WAR IN EAST TENNESSEE—RECEPTION OF GENERAL BURNSIDE BY THE UNIONISTS OF KNOXVILLE.—[See next Page.]

**THE WAR IN EAST TENNESSEE—RECEPTION OF GENERAL BURNSIDE BY THE UNIONISTS OF KNOXVILLE.**

ATTACK ON KNOXVILLE.

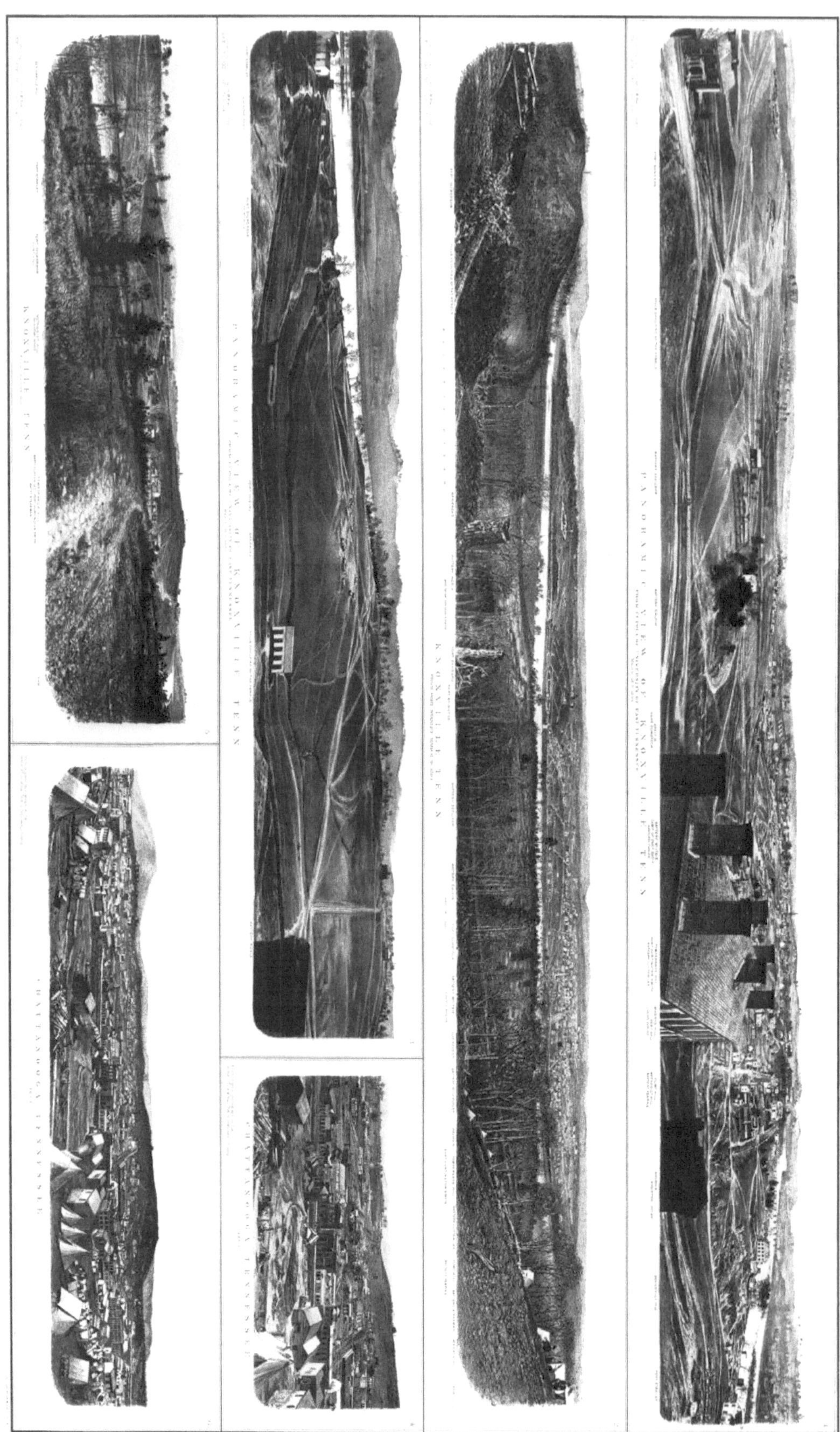

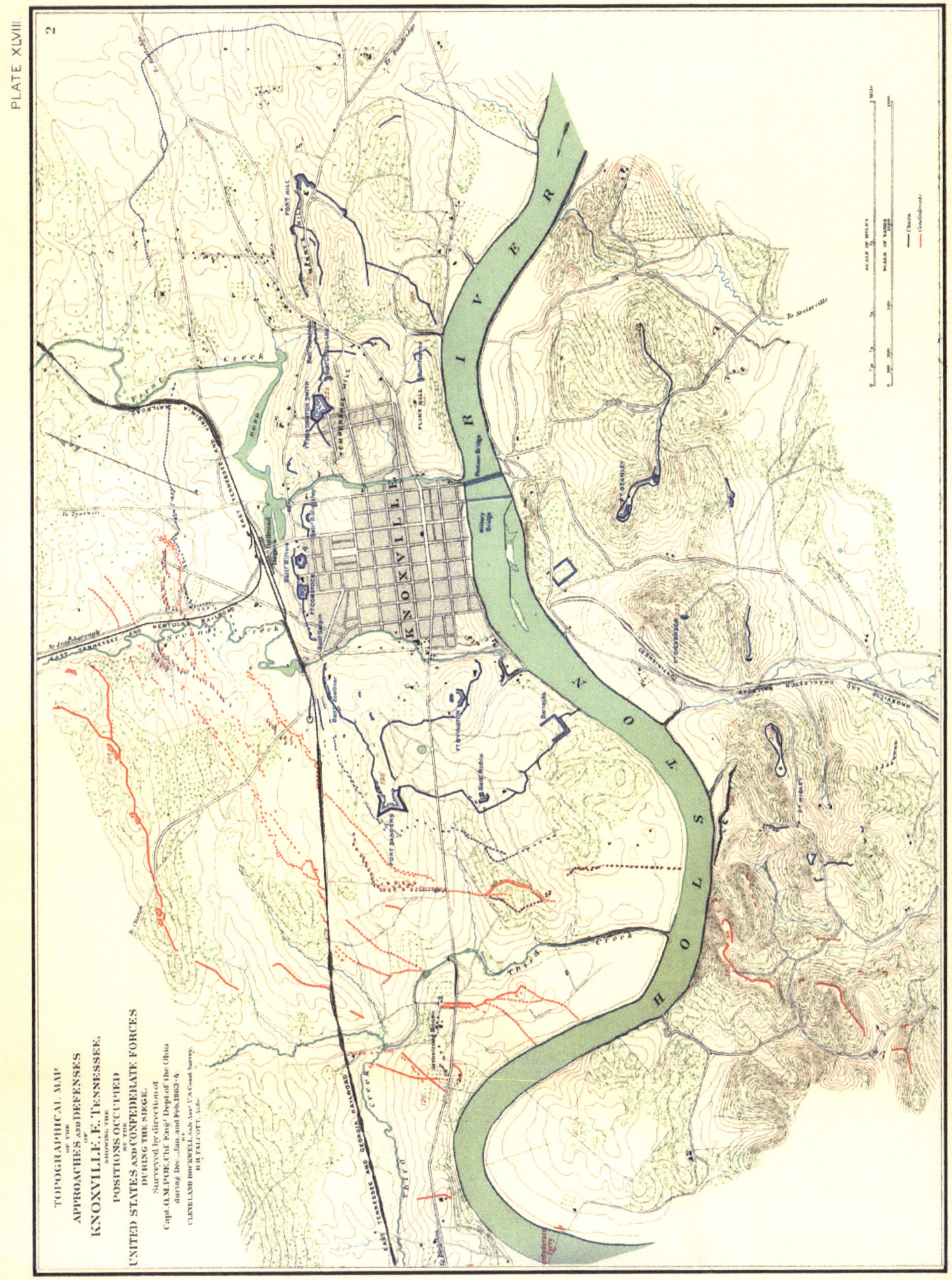

PLATE XLVIII.

2

# TOPOGRAPHICAL MAP
OF THE
## APPROACHES AND DEFENSES
OF
## KNOXVILLE, E. TENNESSEE,
SHOWING THE
## POSITIONS OCCUPIED
BY THE
## UNITED STATES AND CONFEDERATE FORCES
DURING THE SIEGE.

Surveyed by direction of
Capt. O. M. POE, Chf. Eng^r Dept. of the Ohio
during Dec., Jan. and Feb. 1863-4
BY
CLEVELAND ROCKWELL, Sub Ass^t U.S. Coast Survey,
R. H. TALCOTT, Aide.

KNOXVILLE

HOLSTON RIVER

FORT SANDERS

FORT HILL

FLINT HILL

TEMPERANCE HILL

EAST TENNESSEE AND GEORGIA RAILROAD

EAST TENNESSEE AND VIRGINIA RAILROAD

Third Creek

Military Bridge

Pontoon Bridge

FT. STANLEY

FT. HIGLEY

SCALE OF MILES

SCALE OF YARDS

Union

Confederate

# A MAP OF FORT SANDERS.

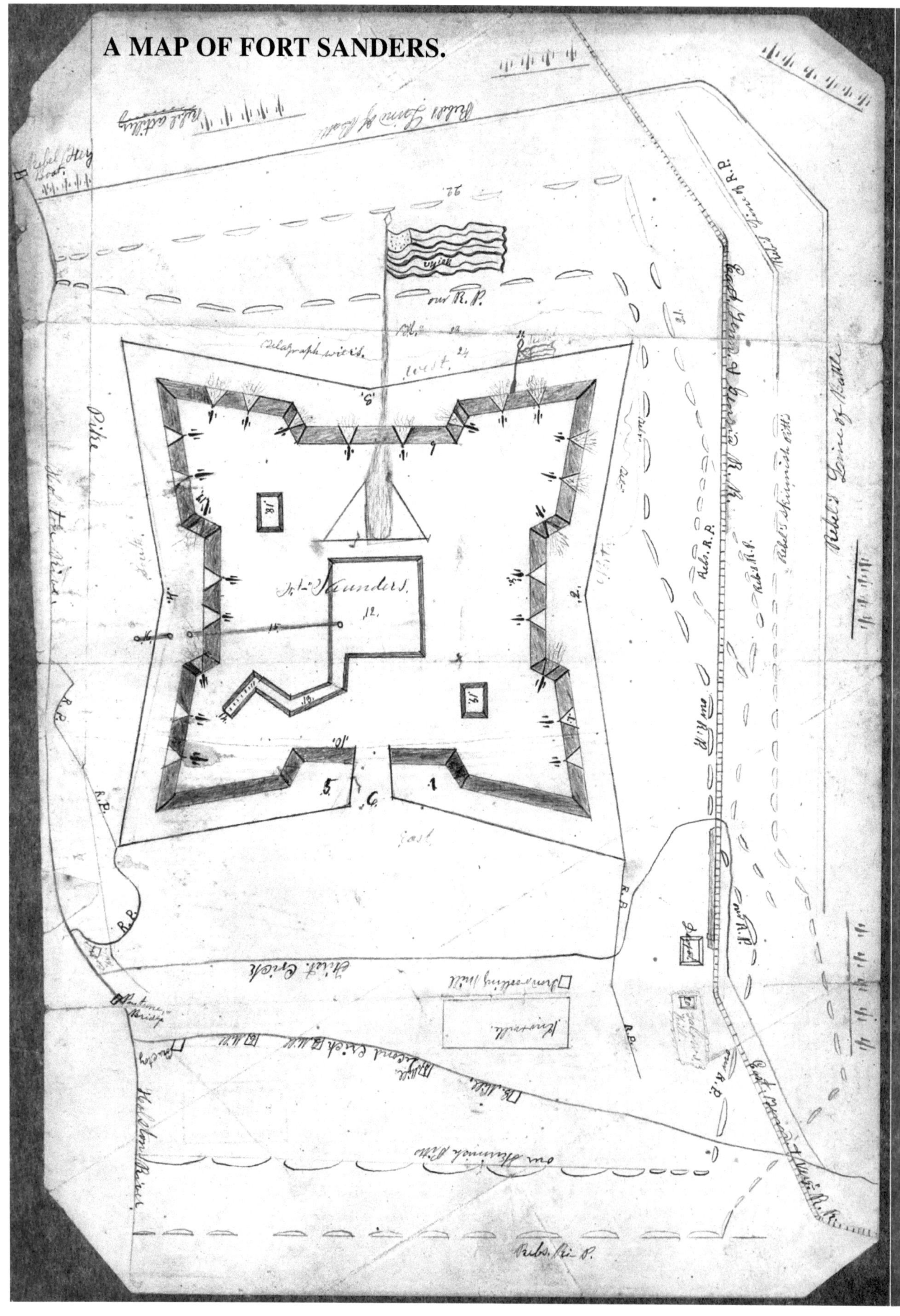

# REBEL WAR REPORTS.

## OPERATIONS IN NORTHERN VIRGINIA—THE DEFEAT BRAGG' S ARMY—ANXIETY CONCERNING LONGSTREET—THE BOMBARDMENT OF CHARLESTON—REPORTS FROM TEXAS AND MEXICO.

### FORTRESS MONROE, Saturday, Dec. 5, 1863.

Copies of The Richmond Enquirer of Dec. 2 and 3, have been received. The following extracts are taken therefrom:

### OPERATIONS IN NORTHERN VIRGINIA. Orange Court-House, Va, Dec. 1, 1863.

Our artillery opened on the enemy yesterday, quite spiritedly. The enemy responded briskly. The artillery duel was kept up all day.

The enemy have thrown up fortifications along the front. Last night they built heavy fires in front, and moved more to our right. One hundred and twenty-seven prisoners were sent to Richmond to-day. Capt. Raine of the Lynchburg Artillery was killed.

### ORANGE COURT-HOUSE, Dec. 2,1863.

There has been no fighting to-day.

The enemy still make a show on our front, but are believed to be falling back to recross the Rapidan River without fighting, or they are going to Fredericksburg to winter.

### THE DEFEAT OF BRAGG'S ARMY. Atlanta, Nov. 28, 1863.

Bragg's headquarters are at Ringgold. The enemy seem disposed to push what they have gained energetically. The battle will be resumed in a day or two between Ringgold and Dalton. The enemy gained what they fought for. Many field and regimental officers are arriving wounded. Great fears are entertained for the safety of Longstreet. Three thousand of the enemy are advancing toward Knoxville.

There is a fight going on at Kingston. Last week Wheeler was ordered there. Firing is heard at London [Loudon].

SECOND DISPATCH.-A train arrived from Dalton this evening, bringing wounded troops. Our forces are still falling back slowly, followed by the enemy.

There was firing all day yesterday.

Bristol, Dec. 2, 1863.

The firing at Knoxville has ceased. The surrender of Burnside is not officially confirmed.

Atlanta, Tuesday, Dec. 1, 1863.

Cleburn's Division engaged Osterhaus one mile this side of Ringgold on Friday, driving him back.

Kelley's Cavalry whipped the enemy at Cleveland on Wednesday.
The enemy are in our front at Ringgold, and our troops are in line of battle, advancing.

Atlanta, Wednesday, Dec. 2, 1863.

The enemy are entrenching themselves at Chickamauga.

There was heavy firing yesterday at Charleston, Tenn.

The enemy burned a portion of Ringgold to-day and retreated, destroying the bridges and railroad track at Chickamauga.

The Yankees hold Cleveland and are advancing on Charleston, Tenn.

**THE BOMBARDMENT OF CERLESTON [Charleston]. CHARLESTON, Nov. 30, 1863.**

The Yankees to-day fired 22 mortar shells at Sumter. One man was killed.

There was much signals during the night with the fleet.

**MORRIS AND BLACK ISLANDS, Dec. 1, 1863.**

The Yankees fired 13 shells at the city last night. Three buildings were struck. The enemy reconnoitered through Pocataligo, carrying off 27 negroes.

SECOND DISPATCH—The enemy fired 16 shells into the city this afternoon. Several buildings were struck. One woman was severely wounded.

There is a lively artillery duel going on between the Gregg batteries and James Island.

DEC. 2, 1863.—The Yankees opened fire on the city this afternoon, and threw six shells. A concentrated fire from our batteries caused them to cease firing.

**REPORTS FROM TEXAS AND MEXICO. MOBILE, Dec. 2, 1863.**

Discouraging accounts are given of desertions in Price's army.

Banks, with 5,000 troops, occupies Brownsville. He did not capture over 50 bales of cotton.

The Mexican guerrilla chief has pronounced against Juarez and the French, and holds Matamoras, increasing the difficulty of trade via the Rio Grande.

**THE WAR. IN THE SOUTH-WEST Rebel Raid on Saulsbury—Gen. Forest Encamped at Rocky Fork with Seventeen Regiments—The Case of Major Devaussee. CAIRO, Saturday, Dec. 5, 1863.**

Memphis papers of the 3d inst. are received.

The Memphis Bulletin says: "Cotton is less active than any day previous to October. The sales to- day were 12 bales."

Forty to fifty Rebels made a raid on Saulsbury on the 2d inst. They tore up the Railroad track for some distance, burning the ties, twisting the rails, and cutting the telegraph wires. Hatch's cavalry started in pursuit of them, and we took forty prisoners and the same number of horses. The Railroad was repaired in twenty-four hours.

A report was brought here last night from Memphis that the Rebel General Forrest was encamped at Rocky Fork, fifteen miles from Holly Springs, on Thursday last, with seventeen regiments, numbering perhaps 8,000 or 10,000 men.

Major Devassee has returned here. He says he can refute the charges against him in regard to defrauding the Government.

Ninety-three Rebel prisoners from Vicksburg were brought up on the Hillman. They will be sent to Indianapolis.

Forty Union deserters from Louisville also arrived.

The steamer Hillman, with sixty-five bales of cotton, had arrived at Cairo.

## FROM NEWBERN, N. C.

The United States steam-transport Ellen S. Terry, Capt. Chapin, arrived on Saturday morning from Newborn, N. C., Dec. 2, and Hatteras Inlet 3d, with the mails and passengers to U. S. Assist. Quarter-master. She brings the following passengers: Mrs. Earle, Lieut. 0. V. Cotter, James B. Otis, A. Collins, G. Dudley, C. H. Otten, and 25 in the steerage.

Capture of Captain White's Guerrillas—Thirteen Large Steamers Run the Blockade of Wilmington.

Correspondence of the Associated Press. Newbern, N. C., Saturday, Nov. 28, 1863.

Capt. Graham, of the 1st North Carolina Union Cavalry, went into the enemy's lines some thirty miles, with his company, on the 25th inst., and surprised and captured Capt. White's entire company of guerrillas, seventy-four in number. They arrived in Newbern this morning. Capt. Graham is the cavalry hero of this Department.

The Raleigh (N. C. Standard of the 20th inst.), contains a dispatch from Wilmington, stating that thirteen large steamers, heavily laden, ran the blockade into Wilmington on the night of the 19th inst.

Raid into the Cherokee Country by Quantrell's Guerrillas. Washington, Saturday, Dec. 3, 1863.

Indian Superintendent Coffin has arrived in this city, bringing to the Indian Bureau an official report concerning a raid made several weeks ago into the Cherokee country by, it is supposed, a party of Quantrell's guerrillas, who destroyed the public buildings at Tamaqua and.the property of the Union citizens, including that of John Ross. The latter's son-in-law was murdered.

Election in Idaho. DENVER City, Saturday, Dec. 5,1863.

Partial returns from the recent election in Idaho indicate that the Hon. John M. Cannaday, Democrat, is elected delegate to Congress by a considerable majority.

## CAPTURE OF THE SHIP "LIVING AGE."

BOSTON, Saturday, Dec. 5, 1863.

The ship "Living Age," which arrived at Falmouth November 17, from Akyab, reports being boarded and bonded by the privateer "Tuescarora," of the Cape of Good Hope.

# New-York  Tribune.

VOL. XXIII....No. 7,071. NEW-YORK, MONDAY, DECEMBER 7, 1863. PRICE THREE CENTS.


## FROM THE MISSISSIPPI DISTRICT.

The Burnside Relief Expedition.

The Reported Death of Breckinridge Confirmed.

THE RETREAT OF BRAGG.

A Severe Fight and Heavy Loss at Ringgold.

Heroic Bravery and Success of Our Troops.

LIST OF OUR CASUALTIES.

SPLENDID RESULTS OF THE LATE VICTORIES.

Large Captures of Arms and Prisoners

PROSPECTS OF A NEW CAMPAIGN.

The Enemy Thoroughly Routed and Demoralized.

CINCINNATI, Saturday, Dec. 5, 1863.

*The Gazette* has the following dispatch:

CHATTANOOGA, Friday, Dec. 4, 1863.

Everything is quiet along the entire line.

Our casualties in the late battle were 4,500.

We captured 6,450 prisoners, and 40 guns.

### The Retreat of Bragg—The Rout and the Pursuit—Artillery and Prisoners Taken —A Severe Fight and Heavy Loss at Ringgold.

From Our Special Correspondent.

BATTLEFIELD, RINGGOLD, Ga., Nov. 27, 1863.

After the shattered and panic-stricken forces of Bragg were driven from Missionary Ridge, Sherman of the 15th Army Corps, was ordered to follow up and harass him on the left, with a portion of the 11th, 15th, and 14th Corps, and Hooker to follow him on the Woodberry and Ringgold dirt road, while Gen. Palmer of the 14th Army Corps was to make for his center. Sherman started about 1 o'clock p. m. of the 25th, and on reaching Chickamauga Creek he found the bridge had been burned and the enemy making fast time toward Ringgold and Dalton. Sherman dispatched immediately to Gen. Grant for instructions as to the best mode of procedure, and it was quickly determined to throw a pontoon across the creek and follow Bragg. This caused considerable delay. Gen. Jeff. C. Davis of Gen. Palmer's Division was in the advance of the 11th and 15th Corps, and succeed in saving a large quantity of corn, rice meal and other commissary stores at Chickamauga Station. The Rebels set fire to everything in their rear, but our advance was in such close proximity to their rear that we saved a good deal of property which might have otherwise been destroyed. There must have been at least 75,000 bushels of corn and meal preserved. About dark Gen. John Beatty and Col. Dan McCook's Brigade of Davis's Division came upon a large body of the enemy's cavalry and infantry, drawn up in line of battle, when both our brigades were brought into line and advanced on the enemy, who was covered by a thick belt of woods, while our forces had to advance through an open field. This lasted an hour and a half. We in the mean time drove the enemy. Seeing that there was no other alternative, the Rebels set fire to their wagons and ingloriously fled toward Greysville. The wagons set on fire were filled with ammunition, but our men succeeded in putting out the fire before any damage was done. While we were engaging and harassing the enemy's rear, Gen. Palmer on the center pushed on at his best speed with Johnson's and Baird's divisions of his corps, and succeeded in reaching Greysville as the enemy were setting the bridge on fire. They had it fired in four places as ...

## THE FIGHT AT CAMPBELL'S STATION.

WOODS

REBELS

BATTERY

LENOIR ROAD

REBELS

KINGSTON ROAD

BATTERIES

CORN FIELD

REBELS

REBEL ADVANCED BATTERY

CORN FIELD

STREAM

PART OF NINTH ARMY CORPS GEN. POTTER

WOODS

GEN. POTTER

BENJAMINS & EDWARDS BATTERIES

BUCKLEYS BATTERY

ROMERS & VON SEHLENS BATTERIES

RESERVES RESERVES

FERRO'S NINTH ARMY CORPS GEN. POTTER

CAVALRY

KNOXVILLE ROAD

WOODS

THE SECOND LINE WAS FORMED ON THIS HEIGHT

lanta Railroad. He will probably succeed in gathering the fragments of his army there.

*The pursuit of Bragg will not continue far*, solely on the ground of supplies and transportation. It is absolutely impossible. Bragg owes the escape of the fragments of his army solely to the fact that there is not forage enough in the country to feed our cavalry, which was not ordered to pursue on that account. It may be difficult for the distant reader to understand this; and some may be disposed to be dissatisfied because the pursuit is not kept up, when the fact is, it is a stroke of generalship not to pursue, under circumstances such as now surround us. Besides, Bragg is thoroughly smashed, and there is very little game left in him or his army. A blow has been struck, the moral effect of which will be tremendous on the South. The next blow will follow in good time and in the right place. The arm that dealt this has undiminished strength.

Without anybody to annoy their flanks, Grant and Thomas will now be free to turn their attention to making this the depot for future operations, which will be postponed not a day longer than is practicable to resume them. Tennessee is now permanently free from the Rebels, for what force there may have been opposed to Burnside will make good their exit soon or not at all.

Among the immediate consequences of this great achievement will be practically a large increase of Grant's force. I presume Burnside will soon effect a junction, while the large force heretofore protecting our right flank having been in a great measure relieved, no small part of it will probably be added to the main body. This concentration is not among the least considerable results of the victory. It renders available another army of no mean proportions with which to deal the next blow.

Prisoners continue to come in hourly. They all tell the same story. Many of them openly curse Bragg, and say that his army has the same feeling.

The number of pieces of artillery captured, though not as large as has been reported, is yet larger than was first supposed. To-day the inventory is forty pieces, including a full battery of the celebrated Washington Artillery of New-Orleans. Of small-arms there will be a very large number—somewhere from six to ten thousand ...

### THE SIEGE OF KNOXVILLE.

The Attack on Fort Sanders—Desperate Struggle by Longstreet—Thrilling Details of the Fighting—Heroic Courage of Our Troops—Complete Failure of the Attack—The City of Knoxville Saved.

Special Dispatch to the Chicago Tribune.

CINCINNATI, Dec. 3, 1863.

Captain W. Anderson, Assistant Adjutant-General, Department of the Ohio, has received the following official dispatch:

KNOXVILLE, Nov. 30,
Via CUMBERLAND GAP, Dec. 2d, 1863.

The enemy attacked us early this morning in force, but we repulsed them with considerable loss. All is well.

A. E. BURNSIDE, Major General.

Special Dispatch to the Chicago Tribune.

KNOXVILLE, Nov. 30, 1863.

The great rebel blow, anxiously anticipated so long, was struck yesterday morning. Reënforced by the troops of Sam Jones, Jackson and Williams, Longstreet sought to annihilate the Army of the Ohio by *coup de guerre*. He selected seven picked regiments.

Skirmishing commenced on Sunday night at ten o'clock, and continued sharply until near daylight of Monday on our left front before Fort Sanders, commanded by Gen. Ferrero and defended by the 79th New-York, Benjamin's 3d U. S. Artillery, and Buckley's Rhode Island Battery.

Our pickets were driven in and the enemy had possessed themselves of some rifle-pits, but the Massachusetts boys drove them back, when suddenly the Rebel storming party, led by the 13th and 17th Georgia and 13th Mississippi, under cover of our own retreating men, came to the assault.

They approached to within one hundred yards of the fort unharmed. Then commenced a series of desperate ...

### REBEL WAR REPORTS.

...

### THE WAR IN THE SOUTH-WEST.

...

Fork, fifteen miles from Holly Springs, on Thursday last, with seventeen regiments, numbering perhaps 8,000 or 10,000 men.

Major Devassee has returned here. He says he can refute the charges against him in regard to defrauding the Government.

Ninety-three Rebel prisoners from Vicksburg were brought up on the Hillman. They will be sent to Indianapolis.

Forty Union deserters from Louisville also arrived.

The steamer Hillman, with sixty-five bales of cotton, had arrived at Cairo.

### FROM NEWBERN, N. C.

The United States steam-transport Ellen S. Terry, Capt. Chapin, arrived on Saturday morning from Newbern, N. C., Dec. 2, and Hatteras Inlet 3d, with the mails and passengers to U. S. Assist. Quartermaster. She brings the following passengers: Mrs. Earle, Lieut. O. V. Cotter, James E. Otis, A. Collins, G. Dudley, C. H. Otten, and 25 in the steerage.

### Capture of Captain White's Guerrillas—Thirteen Large Steamers Run the Blockade of Wilmington.

Correspondence of the Associated Press.

NEWBERN, N. C., Saturday, Nov. 28, 1863.

Capt. Graham, of the 1st North Carolina Union Cavalry, went into the enemy's lines some thirty miles, with his company, on the 25th inst., and surprised and captured Capt. White's entire company of guerrillas, seventy-four in number. They arrived in Newbern this morning. Capt. Graham is the cavalry hero of this Department.

*The Raleigh* (N. C. *Standard* of the 20th inst., contains a dispatch from Wilmington, stating that thirteen large steamers, heavily laden, run the blockade into Wilmington on the night of the 19th inst.

### Raid into the Cherokee Country by Quantrell's Guerrillas.

WASHINGTON, Saturday, Dec. 5, 1863.

Indian Superintendent Coffin has arrived in this city, bringing to the Indian Bureau an official report concerning a raid made several weeks ago into the Cherokee country by, it is supposed, a party of Quantrell's guerrillas, who destroyed the public buildings at Tamaqua and the property of the Union citizens, including that of John Ross. The latter's son-in-law was murdered.

### Election in Idaho.

DENVER CITY, Saturday, Dec. 5, 1863.

Partial returns from the recent election in Idaho indicate that the Hon. John M. Cannaday, Democrat, is elected delegate to Congress by a considerable majority.

## LATEST FROM GEN. BURNSIDE'S ARMY

Gen. Foster Drives the Rebels from Clinch River.

Gen. Longstreet Secures His Retreat.

BATTLE OF CAMPBELL'S STATION.

THE ENEMY TWICE REPULSED.

Only 5,000 Men Hold Longstreet's Army at Bay.

"The Prettiest Little Fight of the War."

RETREAT TO KNOXVILLE.

SIEGE OF THE CITY.

FIGHT OF THE KINGSTON ROAD.

DEATH OF GEN. SANDERS.

THE ENEMY SHELL KNOXVILLE.

Disastrous Sortie by the 20th Michigan.

GOOD NEWS RECEIVED FROM GRANT.

GENERAL BURNSIDE SAFE AT LAST.

Lists of the Killed and Wounded in the Various Actions.

CINCINNATI, Saturday, Dec. 5, 1863.

*The Commercial* has received the following dispatch:

CUMBERLAND GAP, Dec. 4, 1863.

Gen. Foster has driven the enemy from Clinch River, and is in pursuit of him.

The check our forces received yesterday, however, will doubtless secure the retreat of Gen. Longstreet.

### The Fight at Campbell's Station.

From Our Special Correspondent.

CAMPBELL'S STATION, Monday, Nov. 16, 1863.

Learning that the enemy had completed his pontoon below London, and had crossed a considerable force, Gen. Burnside, on the 14th, ordered forward the 2d Brigade of Gen. White's Division. His 1st Brigade had been ordered to Kingston several days previously. This force was accompanied by Gen. Ferrero's Division of the 9th A. C. The enemy's pickets were met and driven in three miles from London. General White directed Col. Chapin, who commanded the brigade, to deploy the 111th Ohio and the 13th Kentucky on the left. General White took charge of the 107th Illinois, deploying it on the right. The regiment gave three cheers for Illinois, and charged into their first fight on the double-quick driving the enemy in confusion from the field. The whole line then pressed steadily forward through the woods skirting the river; the enemy repeated by attempting to make a stand, but as often being dislodged by the steady charge of the line. The 107th Illinois and the 13th Kentucky distinguished themselves. The enemy's loss was large, leaving his dead and wounded on the field. Prisoners, representing five different regiments of Longstreet's corps, were captured. Night compelled a halt within three-quarters of a mile from ...

track, falls away in an abrupt descent of 30 feet at an angle of 45 degrees. This bluff is crowned by rifle-pits along the crest, with logs for the protection of the mens' heads. The left of the hill, to where it slopes more gradually toward the level of the railroad track, is strongly protected by batteries of cotton bales and earth. Here is Edward's fine battery of rifled guns belonging to Col. Siegfried's brigade. To the right of Gay street, which runs from the river north to the railroad, a strong battery also of cotton bales and earth is established. The street is barricaded by wagons and bales of cotton. Rifle-pits also extend right and left across a narrow plateau ending at First Creek. To-day, at noon, this last-named battery opened upon a party who were noticed on the opposite hills planting some guns in position, and obliged them to withdraw. The Rebels, however, first fired three or four shots into the town, at the battery, which fell doing no damage, though they produced some slight "stir." One or two of these missiles passed over the roof of the house where your correspondent was engaged in chronicling events, and suggested the query in his man whether it was a safe place for permanent board.

These half-dozen shots are all that have thus far been fired into the town. I constantly hear it asked by citizens, will General Longstreet get up a general bombardment of the town without first giving timely notice, and permitting non-combatants (your correspondent is among them), with the women and children—like their society—to withdraw. I reply, certainly not. Is not General Longstreet an officer of the *Regular* Army, and will he do so irregular a thing? Is he not a gentleman, a soldier, and, for aught I know, a Christian, and will he slaughter innocent women and children without giving them due notice? Certainly not. Besides, are there not hundreds of the best friends the Southern Confederacy ever had still living in the town, and praying for his success? Thus I endeavor to console the people, and keep them quiet, of course feeling perfectly calm *myself*, and having not the slightest apprehension of danger. Whether these assurances have any effect or not, I observe much more quiet in the town than could have been expected.

Gen. Burnside frequently visits all parts of the line in person, but to insure instantaneous communication between the extremes of the lines and his own headquarters, a telegraph wire has been stretched through the town from Fort Sanders, on Tape Hill, the west front, to Temperance and Mayberry Hills, connecting with headquarters. The same line connects with Col. Cameron's position, crossing the pontoon bridge. The signal flag stations are also located on the most prominent points, having a view of the whole field, and transmitting from one point to the other prompt intelligence of the enemy's movements.

The enemy gradually advanced his skirmishers around toward the center of our position, taking advantage of a belt of woods, on higher ground than that occupied by ours, and crept up to a thin grove of oak and pine skirting the woods. Edward's battery fired an occasional shot at the party observed on an opposite hill engaged in building earth works for a battery.

WHAT THE ENEMY IS DOING—HIS POSITION.

While we have a strong position—strong by nature, and strengthened by the best engineering skill—the enemy has also great advantages for attack; and, aside from the question of food for men and animals, he no doubt regards the capture of the place as only a work of time. Lest, in any untoward event, our brave army and its commander should be improperly criticized, I ought to describe the situation more fully. The enemy's right at present rests on the river, his forces finding ample protection among the hills and valleys through which runs the Kingston road toward the south-west. The whole country is hilly. The direction of the hills is generally at right angles to the river, obliging us to hold those clear to the bank of the stream, lest the enemy should come up under its cover to turn our flank. If possible, I have no doubt he will cross below and endeavor to occupy a high range of hills which we could not conveniently take possession of. Toward their left, the hills, or a part of them, are high, and all have a growth, more or less dense, of timber, which, to a great degree, conceal their movements from observation. Occasionally we obtain glimpses through the partial openings of bodies of cavalry passing. The enemy to-day have evidently been looking out favorable positions for locating batteries. In an air-line of an average distance of a mile from Edward's Battery, Sigfried's command, is a line of hills gradually rising from the enemy's left to a high point north-west by west of the town. That point is higher than the bluff on which the last-named battery is located. A plateau intervenes occupied by farms, crossed by fence inclosures in different directions, and through which run the Clinton Railroad, the country road to the same place, and that to Tazewell. Still back of this high land is a country by-road on which we see their wagons and artillery passing. This road intersects the Tazewell road at a distance of say two miles from the north side of the town. From about our center, nearly to the extreme right, the country is more level and open, with only scattering clumps of pines and scrub oaks. Here, then, are no positions favorable for batteries within a mile of ours. From our line the view is comparatively unobstructed. Still further round, the country becomes more hilly, and wooded hills and valleys extend to the Holston River, leaving one open space only on the extreme right, occupied by farms.

The 19th closes warm, with a hazy atmosphere. S. A.

### A Charge and a Conflagration—Shelling the City—Brilliant Sortie of the 17th Michigan—Rain.

From our Special Correspondent.

KNOXVILLE, Nov. 20—Morning.

A smoky atmosphere obscures the fort and conceals the enemy's position and movements. There is an occasional shot from the pickets on either side, until 9 o'clock, when it cleared off, and the picket firing became quite general, particularly along the center, on the Clinton and Tazewell roads. The skirmishers occupy nearly the same position as last evening at half a mile from our fortified line. The enemy's sharpshooters keep behind trees or fallen logs, and sometimes dig a hole in the ground from which they take aim at our pickets.

A CHARGE AND A CONFLAGRATION.

About 10 o'clock a sudden discharge of musketry attracted attention at the center of our line. Our pickets advanced upon those of the enemy who had concealed themselves in a frame-house, and were annoying them. It was the residence of Mr. Brannan, brother of the President of Ocoll Bank. It was set on fire, and soon burned to the ground. Skirmishing continued with more or less activity until 5 p. m., when there was a sudden cessation of firing. The Rebel pickets withdrew, as was supposed, for a night attack. Our pickets fell back, firing the buildings they had occupied during the day. They were a large brick dwelling and out-buildings located in the plain on the line occupied by our skirmishers, and two or three buildings in the scattered portion of the village beyond the railroad. It was intended as a measure of precaution, but they were prematurely fired. The buildings being in range of our batteries and rifle-pits, it may become necessary also to destroy a large portion of the railroad buildings and the houses contiguous to prevent them from being used as a cover for the enemy's sharpshooters. A few moments before the conflagration the enemy opened a battery near the front of our center, and fired four or five shots into the town. They were apparently aimed at the Cotton-bale Battery on Gay street. The missiles, as they came whizzing into town, caused considerable panic, and for a few moments the impression prevailed among the citizens that the grand shelling had begun. The Gay street battery, as well as two others to the right and left, replied rapidly, their reports shaking the town. Spectators went skurrying for shelter to the neighboring buildings; teams skedaddled up Gay street, and citizens took to their cellars for protection. For some cause the Rebel batteries ceased firing, probably from a fear of hurting somebody in the town—ours followed suit—and there was a great calm. Meantime the heavens were illuminated by the lurid flames of the burning buildings, attracting a crowd of the more venturesome to Summit Hill to witness the scene. The spectacle was grand and imposing to those who had never witnessed a conflagration in New-York. These frequent illuminations seem to indicate that the entertainment coming off is to be got up without regard to expense. But seriously, nothing but the most urgent necessities of war, and such I suppose now existed, could justify the destruction of these houses. As covers for the Rebel sharpshooters (they are within easy rifle range of our batteries) they would be fatal to the occupation and working of our batteries. The less, therefore, must be sacrificed to the greater.

Aside from this episode affairs soon became quiet. I omitted to mention that one of the shells fell in the yard of Gen. Burnside's headquarters, from which, however, he and his staff had moved during the day.

BRILLIANT SORTIE OF THE SEVENTEENTH MICHIGAN.

At 6½ p. m. rapid cannonading was heard on our right front—Fort Sanders—which roused the town from its temporary repose. Now, it was supposed the expected night attack had begun. The advance, it seems, was by our side, and not from that of the enemy. The Rebel pickets, during the day, had got into James Armstrong's house, just under the hill, and had very much annoyed our men. Gen. Ferrero accordingly ordered the 17th Michigan to make a sortie and drive them out. The work was handsomely accomplished, and the house set on fire. They then fell back; but as the light of the burning buildings burst forth it revealed the position of our men as they were deploying into the road, and the enemy swept their ranks by discharges of shell and solid shot. One Lieutenant was killed and three men wounded. Our batteries replied as fast as possible, covering our men as they retreated. The object was accomplished, though after sacrifice of valuable men, and the Michigan boys deserve much praise for the handsome manner in which they executed their task. The combined detonations of our own and the Rebel guns shook the town to its center, and citizens rushed into the streets to ascertain what was up. Some of the Rebel shells, passing over the fort on Tape Hill, fell in the streets of the town, causing some alarm. For a long time the people watched the light of the blazing dwelling, but the batteries ceased firing, the flames gradually died out, and there was another great calm. The night passed without any other general alarm.

*November 20.*—During the latter part of the night rain began to fall heavily, and continued until 2 o'clock p. m. The country has been thoroughly drenched, and traveling on the roads impeded. The picket firing seems to be working around to the right. The evident intention of the enemy is to feel of our whole position before making the final attack. The rain, which is uncomfortable for both sides, must be particularly unfavorable for the Rebels, who have not yet got their guns in position or their works complete. Ours, luckily, were finished before the rain set in.

*Nov. 21, Evening.*—The afternoon has been clear, with a bracing atmosphere—wind from the north-west. The enemy's pickets are about in the same position as yesterday, but the firing has not been active. Two or three have come in wounded. General Manson gave the enemy two shots from his batteries on Temperance Hill, directed to the battery to the left oblique, but no response was elicited. There are rumors and reports of the enemy crossing a force over the Holston, below, with a view of attacking Cameron's position on Flint Hill.

### Progress of the Siege.

From Our Special Correspondent.

KNOXVILLE, Tenn., Nov. 22, 1863.

The siege of Knoxville is progressing, it is presumed, according to the most approved principles of warfare. Outside, the enemy keeps his skirmishers busy. He builds batteries, fells trees, constructs redoubts, and occasionally fires a shell into town, at some one of our batteries. Inside, our forces lie in their rifle-pits or behind their well-constructed batteries, and watch the movements of the enemy. We are also indefatigable in strengthening the works of defense already constructed, and in extending them where they are needed. Every hour adds to the impregnability of the town against assault.

The morning dawned clear, with a bracing atmosphere, and the day has been one of the finest we have experienced for weeks. The roads are already fast drying, and traveling is getting passable. The enemy has been busy in the front of Summit Hill—which is the highest and most favorable position for artillery—and this morning reveals a large cleared space, two strong earthworks, and a line of rifle-pits around the crest of the hill, the whole at a distance of one mile in an air line. Their camp smoke has disappeared from the north side of the town, and a large column is visible at the southwest, in the direction of where the chief attack was made on Tuesday, showing that they have their chief forces in that direction. To-day the respective pickets occupy about the same position as yesterday. There has been a brief truce between the enemy's pickets and those of the 11th New Hampshire, and some pleasant raillery passing between them yesterday and to-day. "Have you got old Burnside in there?" "How comes on his 'rear'?" "Have you had any mail lately?" "How are you Vicksburg?" "Got plenty of mule meat on hand?" and such like queries, come from the Rebel side, and are answered according to the whim of the Union pickets. They attempt to make us think they have captured one of our inward bound mails, which is quite likely; that they have captured "old Brownlow," which is n't likely, as he telegraphed "all safe" from Cumberland Ford a week ago; that they have captured his press, which we know was not started from Cincinnati, and various other things calculated to annoy us. The Rebels threw several shells at the battery on Temperance Hill about sunset, from the battery which I have already described—the range of fire being obliquely to the river front of the town—i. e., from north-west to south-east nearly. One of the enemy's shells severely wounded a cavalry man who was standing in a group to the rear of the battery. His lower jaw was carried away.

At 7 o'clock our battery opened upon the enemy's position and fired some half a dozen rounds. There was no reply, and up to the present time, 6½ p. m., everything remains quiet. There is a bright moonlight, which is favorable to the operations of the enemy, but there is some expectation of a night attack on the town. S. A.

KILLED AND WOUNDED AT THE SORTIE NIGHT OF NOV. 20.

Private Joseph Leonard, Co. F, 17th Mich., skull fractured by shell. Dead.

WOUNDED WHILE SKIRMISHING NOV. 19TH, 20TH AND 21ST.

2d Lieut. Alvin M. Reed, Co. D, 100 P. V., flesh wound of both legs.

Wm. Cole, Co. I, 50th P. V., skull fractured.

Corp. Phineas Bird, Co. C, 100 P. V., fracture of skull.

Corp. Conrad Homan, Co. A, 29th Mass., flesh wound, right hand.

Private Jno. A. Connesty, Co. G, 100th P. V., right leg amputated above knee.

Private Jno. W. Rodgers, Co. H, 100th Pennsylvania Volunteers, fracture of upper portion of arm; resection performed.

Private Robert Burns, Co. G, 29th Massachusetts, flesh wound of shoulder and fracture of lower jaw; severe.

*Monday, Nov. 23, 7½ a. m.*—Morning pleasant, but smoky on the hills. No sign of an attack. Everything in readiness and troops in good spirits. S. A.

### Arrival of Couriers from Cumberland Gap—Cheering News—A Reconnoissance—Flag Raising—The Enemy Turned Back—Another Fire—Sortie by the 20th Michigan—Its Disastrous Failure—List of Killed and Wounded—Death of Gen. Sanders.

From Our Special Correspondent.

KNOXVILLE, Tenn., Nov. 23, 1863.

Having finished and inclosed to you a history of events up to this morning, I begin a new chapter with the beginning of this week. The day has been still, Summer-like, and so warm in the sun as to be uncomfortable. Out of some eight or ten couriers sent

# BIBLIOGRAPHY.

These sources are in the personal library of Charles A. Reeves, Jr., with exceptions as noted.

Page 1 - Engraving of Burnside - *The American Soldier in the Civil War,* Frank Leslie, 1985, p. 497.

Page 2 - The Fight at Campbell's Station Map - This newspaper article.

Page 3 - ***Battle of Campbell Station*** - painting by Paul J. Long.

Page 5 - Engraving of Sanders - *The Defense of Knoxville,* Orlando M. Poe, published in 1886 as part of The Century Magazine's *Battles and Leaders of the Civil War* series, p. 740.

Page 8 - Engraving of Bragg - Leslie, p. 474.

Page 9 - ***Battle of Chattanooga,*** Kurz & Allen, 1891, print at the Library of Congress.

Page 11 - ***Battle of Chattanooga,*** Kurz & Allen.

Page 13 - ***Battle of Chickamauga,*** Kurz & Allen.

Page 16 - Engraving of Longstreet - Leslie, p. 57.

Page 19 - ***Assault on Fort Sanders,*** Kurz & Allen.

Page 33 - ***Map of Immediate Vicinity of Fort Sanders,*** Poe, p. 739.

Page 33 - Engraving, ***Confederate Assault on Fort Sanders,*** Poe, p. 731.

Page 34 - Engravings, Poe, pp. 738, 747, 749.

Page 35 - ***Longstreet's Assault on Fort Sanders,*** *Harper's Pictorial History of the Civil War,* November 186?.

Page 36 - ***The War in East Tennessee—Reception of General Burnside by the Unionists of Knoxville,*** *Harper's Weekly,* October 24, 1863, front cover.

Page 37 - ***Attack on Knoxville,*** a copy by Johnson Fry & Co. in 1868, of an original painting by Nast.

Page 38 - ***Scenes of Knoxville,*** *The Atlas to Accompany the Official Records of the Union and Confederate Armies,* George B. Davis, et. al., 1891-1895.

Page 39 - ***Topographical Map of the Approaches and Defenses of Knoxville...,*** Davis, p. 130 (a color 17" x 22" version of this map is available from ReevesMaps.com [CAR-MAP-164]).

Page 40 - ***A Map of Fort Sanders,*** John G. Orth, from the American Memory Collection of the Library of Congress, 1863 (a color version of this map is available from ReevesMaps.com [CAR-MAP-253]).

Pages 45-46 - The first (front) and second pages of the subject issue of the *New York Daily Tribune,* December 7, 1863. Donated to the Town of Farragut, TN Folklife Museum.

www.ingramcontent.com/pod-product-compliance
Lightning Source LLC
LaVergne TN
LVHW070153110826
845147LV00002B/392

* 9 7 8 0 9 8 0 0 9 8 4 0 2 *